# ISRAEL, THE ETERNAL IDEAL

# ISRAEL

## the eternal ideal

by Irving Miller

FARRAR, STRAUS AND CUDAHY, *New York*

*To The Memory Of My Father*
*who by precept and example*
*taught me to love my people*

**FOREWORD**

Three thousand years ago a people of shepherds and farmers on the shores of the East Mediterranean evolved ideas of startling originality which have remained the ideal standard of human conduct across the gulf of generations. Rising up in rebellion against the fatalism and resignation of all preceding civilizations, Israel proclaimed the revolutionary doctrines of individual morality, social justice and universal peace.

At the center of Israel's historic experience stands the interpretation of the universal design in terms of order and progress. To vindicate this idea we, the descendants of the ancient Jewish Kingdoms, stubbornly preserved our identity and union for two thousands years of exile until, in our decade, we achieved the restoration of Israel's sovereignty in the aftermath of the Jewish people's most agonizing disaster.

Our modern state is the lineal heir of this long tradition. Israel is not a new Esperanto nation writing its history on a clean slate. The ancient glory inspires both our memory and our ambition. The Biblical literature, the Hebrew language, the pursuit of universal order and progress are the spiritual roots of our nationhood. Seen in this light, the smallness of our state in area and population are enlarged in the consciousness of men by the broad vistas of historic experience. A people small in geography may well be great in history. Modern Israel should be contemplated in historic depth, and not merely in terms of its visible surface.

This is a majestic theme; and Rabbi Miller is its eloquent exponent. All his work and writings in the cause of Israel's resurgence have been illuminated by a reverent perception of Israel as a central idea of history. The reader of this volume will easily come to understand why those who have labored in Israel's cause have been rewarded by the exhilaration of contact with eternity.

*Abba Eban*

July 21, 1955
EMBASSY OF ISRAEL
WASHINGTON, D.C.

# CONTENTS

# INTRODUCTION

This little book is not intended either as a history of the Zionist Movement or of the young State of Israel. It is a primer, as it were, which attempts to explain the age-old origins and fresh events which gave rise to the rebirth of a nation and its land.

What I have endeavored to show is that the State of Israel which came into existence on May 14, 1948, as a result of the authority of the United Nations and through the strength of its own infant arms, was in process of becoming again ever since its dissolution nearly two thousand years ago. For centuries, the dream and the promise, sustained only by faith and prayer, remained dormant until the great liberating impulse, of which our own American Revolution was part, gave them new life.

Transcending the contemporary flux of events and interplay of personalities, the transient conflict of interests and rights, Israel's rebirth represents a triumph for the moral purpose which pervades the true history of man and civilization. In this sense, Israel is much more than one more state playing a lively and sturdy role in the world's affairs. It is the product of centuries of human endurance, ennobled by faith, followed by decades of self-sacrifice by devoted pioneers who set their stamp on the soul and countenance of a reborn Israel.

This glorious theme cannot be fully expounded or done justice within a few pages. It is my hope that by this brief preface to Israel's story there may be stimulated a wider and deeper understanding of the great historical motivation and religious impulse which, in our own times, have restored dignity to the Jewish people as they once again assume their rightful place in the family of nations.

I. M.

ISRAEL, THE ETERNAL IDEAL

# 1    "IF I FORGET THEE. . . ."

On May 14, 1948, a few bold men proclaimed the establishment of the state of Israel, and the nations gasped with disbelief. Human epics mount to their climaxes along the crest of long waves of struggle. Mankind's gaze is focused on the spectacle of the surge of history, and seldom observes the countless tiny eddies in time and eternity.

Yet here it was at last, a living fact again after the innumerable ripples of two thousand years: a nation recreated within little more than two generations; a state that had re-emerged from the stormy welter of modern history with its confused pattern of political intrigue and propaganda, hard-headed international inquiry and lofty humanitarian impulse, promise and repudiation, pledge and deceit.

A nation is generally created through the interplay of accident and desire. The accident takes place when a certain group of human beings situated in a certain place discover national homogeneity within natural boundaries. The desire is the search of this group for self-expression and self-determination. Language, custom, and culture, indigenous to the same people living on the same land, create and mould a national ethos which in turn makes a nation.

The historical pattern, however, is radically different with regard to the citizens in the case of the little country called Israel. Relatively few of its inhabitants were born there. Most of its citizens came from all over the world. They brought with them a bewildering confusion of customs, languages and cultures. The hills and the valleys, the rivers and the plains of the land did not mould them into one folk. Indeed, they understood little about the desert or the sea surrounding their promised land. Only their Jewish identity gave them homogeneity. And only this land and their yearning to recreate themselves in it moulded them into a nation.

It is not always obvious what it is that makes the Jew. There are those who hold that a Jew is a member of an undefined fraternity. Others contend that some racial similarity determines a Jew. To still others, cultural affinity determines the nature of the Jew. Finally, some find in a common history and in the belief in one God the fundamental roots of Jewish existence. Certainly, to insist that only one single or an inflexible combination of several factors defines a Jew would still exclude many who call themselves such. And yet, Jewishness involves an interweaving of many sacred and secular strands. Judaism, it would appear, involves a knowledge of God, the universe and man, a personal and social morality, sacred acts and observances, a code of law, a divine literature, institutions through which these find expression, and the people itself. All are vital elements in the spirit of eternal Israel.

Entwined through centuries of expression and use, these strands have been woven into the fabric of Judaism which has granted creative and meaningful life to the many generations of Israel. There are Jews who do not observe the Commandments; who are unfamiliar with the sacred literature; whose views of the nature of the universe differ from those of traditional Judaism. These differences, however, do not exclude them from participating in the existence of the Jewish people. Only utter indifference to the fact of being a Jew might deny a Jew his Jewishness. But then he may find to his cost that the outside world may impose it on him.

"The greatest proof of your Jewishness," explained one rabbi to a member of his congregation, "is when you live in and with the hopes, and aspirations, the traditions and memories of your people."

The nineteenth century pioneers who migrated to Palestine fervently repeated the old Biblical pledge, "If I forget thee O Jerusalem, let my right hand forget her cunning." It was from Holy City and Holy Land that hope and tradition streamed forth. And it was their people, cruelly banished from that same land two thousand years before, whose ideals they professed. With their return, the pioneers affirmed their aspiration to redeem the land.

Jewish memory goes back to the days when Moses led his people out of bondage in Egypt to receive the Law at Sinai, and to reach the very gates of the promised land.

The first two thousand years of Jewish history are vibrant, vivid histories of kings and prophets, with the glory of two Temples built to one God, with pang of war and sorrow of famine, with the joy of peace and the comfort of prosperity. During those centuries the spirit of Israel evolved and took shape.

The advent of the Roman Empire marked the beginning of the end for the Jewish national state. The Romans had swept over Europe and into western Asia. In Europe they established civilization, but in Asia they looted and conquered and reduced their victims to vassalage. The Roman rulers feuded among themselves, and while civil war raged in Rome, their proconsuls in the Holy Land changed four different times. Each new prefect was worse than his predecessor. Each administration was stained with bloodshed. One Roman governor summarily sold thirty thousand Jews into slavery. Rebellion was the inevitable reaction.

In 39 B.C.E. Rome elevated the despotic Herod to the throne of Palestine. Guerrilla warfare again broke out. In Galilee thousands of Jews fought in the hills until the Roman legions flushed them out and slaughtered them. Jerusalem was besieged; the Romans slew the Jewish rebels until they wearied of the carnage. For a while Herod made an effort to pacify the rebellious people. He erected a glittering marble temple for them. But it served him little; the Jews hated him as much for his own paganism as for his despotism. Before Herod died of a stomach cancer, he plunged the land into another orgy of blood, murdering his wife, his children and almost all who were close to him.

After Herod's death, as though the violence of his rule were incomplete, an earthquake devastated the land. Seven years later came a famine accompanied by plague. For ten years the Jews continued to rebel against Herod's sons. Suppressed without mercy, each outbreak led to more mass executions.

Finally the Romans decided to rule the country directly through Roman rather than native governors. One of them, Pontius Pilate, was in power for ten years. Scornful of the people's religious beliefs, he repeatedly attempted to humiliate them by erecting graven images in public places. These insults would always be followed by violent uprisings, which were just as violently suppressed. In Galilee, the heartland of the religious resistance, Jewish legions mobilized and the great insurrection was under way. In a series of daring and heroic assaults the people attacked Roman camps and communications throughout Palestine.

From Rome, Nero dispatched 50,000 soldiers under Vespasian to subdue the Jewish revolt. By 68 C.E., when Vespasian became emperor and yielded his command to his son, Titus, only Jerusalem still held out.

The Holy City itself was well fortified. Its crowded population vowed to resist until death. Titus' legions drove battering rams against its walls. From a quarter of a mile away a gigantic catapult hurled 125-pound rocks on the defenders. After months of siege, the walls were breached, but although racked by starvation and disease, the people still refused to surrender. They fortified themselves in the Temple; the Temple gates fell. The Roman soldiers burned the holy shrine to the ground and butchered the survivors. Finally, in 70 C.E., the nation lost its land—not with a whimper—but with a solemn cry of defiance.

A time of uneasy peace followed. A half century later, in a final gesture of bravery, the Jews arose against the emperor Hadrian. This time the carnage was meticulously thorough. A half million perished, and most of those who survived were sold into slavery. The wild beasts of the Roman arena devoured the able-bodied. New laws forbade a Jew to live in Jerusalem, and only once a year were Jews permitted to enter the city to weep on the site of the razed Temple. The exile had begun, but from the moment the first tear fell, the hope of redeeming the beloved land was born in Jewish hearts.

The tattered remnants of a nation in exile scattered east and west. In Western Europe the Jews settled in France and England, where they found a brief refuge, and in the Germanic lands. In Spain, they achieved a peak of cultural and material growth. During the Crusades, however, their lot worsened. The soldiers who marched eastward to conquer Palestine for their emperors in the name of their faith attacked every Jewish community in their path, murdering and plundering like the pagans.

In the thirteenth, fourteenth and fifteenth centuries the Jews were driven from England, France and the Iberian Peninsula. Though the Turks, attracted by their talents, invited them to settle in the Ottoman Empire, the Germans, on the other hand, drove them from their lands. Dutch Jews were not allowed to engage in trade until the seventeenth century and did not receive full citizenship until 1796. Throughout the greater part of Europe no Jew was allowed to own land and till the soil.

The story of European Jewry is sad and repetitious. It is the story of the ghetto and its humiliations, tempered by great promise. It is the story of the lure of unreal hope and the abandonment of ancient memory. But it is also the story of return and rebirth in the truth of ancient affirmation.

The beginning of the nineteenth century found the Jewish horizon bright and promising. And yet, not until 1832 did Britain grant enfranchisement to Jews. Norway refused them the right to tread its soil until 1860. Even in Switzerland, with its long tradition of political freedom, the Jews lived in quasi-ghettos and under considerable disabilities until the middle of the nineteenth century. If the early nineteenth century marked the beginning of freedom for Jews of Europe,

the latter part of the century was darkened by the beginnings of new persecutions. In Russia under Alexander III, Cossacks killed and plundered as they rode
through Jewish villages. The terror spread to Central
Europe. Once again the ghetto walls rose with their
soul-shattering humiliation.

History had taught this proud people the meaning of
survival as no other people alive had ever had to learn it.
The Jew endured his pain in silence, saddened that so
few would accord him a crumb of peace on this earth.
In the ghetto he lived in his faith, and by the teachings
of the Torah. But his life was defensive. He might hope
to survive, but to create and to flourish seemed beyond
hope in a universe of hatred. The theme of ghetto culture was grief; its humor self-directed; and the furrowed
brow and the bent back marked the face and body of
European Jewry.

Yet even the walls of a ghetto policed by the cruelest
guards could not forever suppress the striving for
growth that always exists in living minds. The short-
lived enlightenment of the nineteenth century had fired
Jews around the world with new-found courage to liberate themselves. For a time young Austrian Jews became
so adept with the foils that, when reviled by anti-
Semites, they challenged—and won the duel. In Russia,
they began to meet the assaults of the Cossacks with
determined defense measures. They won no wars, only
a few isolated skirmishes. But their actions heralded a
new approach to their travail—to plan bravely and to
fight daringly.

Though history's martyrs, Jews have kept their Messianic faith, never doubting its redemptive promise. But where, and how was this promise—of peace and justice —to be kept? To a Jew who had known the ghetto the answer seemed simple: in a place where a Jew might worship unafraid; where he might earn a livelihood, rear a family and govern himself—there would the promise come true. If modern democracy was born in the turbulence of the French Revolution, its seeds had long before been sown in the suffering hearts of Jews. Tyranny had taught its lesson well. The answer to the question of the past lay in a future inspired by desire for independence. And where better could the Jew find independence? Where but in the land where the Messianic ideal was born.

From the question and the hope there grew a dream worthy of the past and an attitude alive to the need of the present, to the end that the hope for the future would come true. The Jew began to seek the means of his self-deliverance. Out of this search emerged in 1860 the Alliance Israélite Universelle; its aim to unite Jews all over the world and inspire them to stand erect. In 1891, Baron Maurice de Hirsch founded and endowed the Jewish Colonization Society. Still later, he bequeathed most of his fortune toward the aim of resettling Jews in places where they might develop their lives in security. Then came organizations such as the Lovers of Zion who openly declared that the only answer to the Jewish plight lay in a return to the Holy Land.

Colonies established in Argentina, in Brazil, and in Canada floundered and failed. Individuals might prosper in such places; but group settlements were doomed to failure.

The Zionist movement as created by Theodor Herzl best embodied this new spirit of self-deliverance. The movement did not spring from selfish hopes for individual profit. Few of the early Zionists had even seen the land of Israel. While the efforts of de Hirsch and Rothschild depended upon patronage and charity, Zionism insisted on basing itself on the solid ground of self-help. The inspiring force came from the challenge of the land and of the people, for only a redeemed people could redeem their land. In this belief lay the spiritual test and strength of Zionism. The memory that this particular land evoked drew together from all the lands of their dispersal the varied people who called themselves Jews and set them marching in step toward a common goal as they had not marched for two thousand years.

Once immigration to Palestine began in earnest—about the beginning of the 20th century—it never really halted. Two great international wars, changes of regime, interference from occupying powers, hostility from jealous neighbors, physical threats—all failed. An inspired people redeemed a sick and tired land and in so doing redeemed themselves. On May 14, 1948, they announced to the world their re-emergence into history as an independent nation in a sovereign state.

# 2  FORERUNNERS AND PIONEERS

The crowded years of the last half century, during which Israel was recreated, blur the distinctive contributions of the different groups who settled the land. Viewed even in the slight perspective of some fifty years of history, it becomes clear that each of them wove its very special thread into what was to become the fabric of the nation.

At almost all times during the history of the Diaspora, Jews could be found in the Holy Land. There always remained a few—to remember ancient glories, to live in the past, hidden in the shadows of the Wailing Wall and the tragic hillsides. They really did not hope; all they dared was to remember. Through the years, a few stragglers who came but to remember bid the ghettos of Europe a bitter farewell and joined their brothers. They lived mainly in four holy cities, Tiberias, Safed, Hebron and Jerusalem. Knowing little of agriculture, they scratched out a pitiful existence as petty traders and artisans in the urban centers. The little coin boxes in synagogues throughout the world helped them keep their bodies alive; they served, as it were, as the proxies for distant Jews, to salve the conscience of the Diaspora. Of their entire group of 25,000 in the mid-nineteenth century, only six hundred worked on the land. In later years, some few worked the land as they had learned to do at the agricultural school of Mikveh Israel, built by the Alliance Israélite Universelle in 1870.

Each wave of modern Palestinian immigration is known as an *aliyah*—an ascent. The Jews who lived in Palestine until 1881 are not considered as part of an *aliyah*; they happened to be there, their *"ascent"* was from the past.

The modern return to Zion began with the first *aliyah* in 1882, which immediately followed the savage pogroms in Russia. Seven thousand Russian townsfolk, pursuing their accustomed vocations, settled in the cities of Palestine. But within that *aliyah* were twenty unusual pilgrims whose destiny was to mould the character of the entire Zionist movement. They had organized in Kharkov, Russia, a society known as *Chovevei Zion* (Lovers of Zion) and had set sail for Palestine. On board ship, like the Pilgrim Fathers, they wrote a compact vowing to devote themselves to work the soil in cooperative endeavor. Their manifesto proclaimed that they sought a home "in our country" and that they "would beg it of the Sultan." Their declaration ended with the words, "Zion is our only hope."

Their hope in Zion was the land. Older settlers appraised them for what they were, soft-handed young students, intellectuals trying to become peasants, and refused them work. Burning idealism, fired by visions of social justice and the zeal of their compact, sustained them as they dug ditches to support themselves. Undaunted, they stood by their title *Bilu*—derived from the initial letters of the Biblical verse, "House of Jacob, come let us go up" (*Bet ya'akov, l'chu v'nelcha*).

The representative of a colonization society purchased for them a tract of land where they established the first colony of Rishon-le-Zion. However, weary of the loneliness and toil, many departed again. But the ten who remained could not be shaken in their healthy self-confidence despite many misfortunes. The Turkish police harassed them with much petty nastiness. The huts in which they lived together were frequently attacked by marauding Arabs, who had to be fought off with stones and later with firearms. There was not a single plow, and their total equipment consisted of a mule, a gun and some primitive utensils. Their vines took four years to bear fruit. Eventually, years later, through their own fierce determination and some outside aid, the colony prospered. The settlers moved into stone houses, harvested the rich crops of their vineyards, and secured peace for themselves. The attackers stayed away for fear of inciting the wrath of a group which had earned its tenure on the land and would not be displaced.

Their devotion to the cause of rebirth, their sense of complete self-sacrifice fired the imagination of the Diaspora. So much was done with so little. Traditionalists frequently cautioned the impetuous Zionists, "You must not rush the Messiah." To that the dynamic *Biluim* would answer, "We did not rush him at all, we just hurried things up to make the way easier for him."

*Bilu* never won large numbers of followers. Additional *Bilu* groups, usually small in number, followed from Russia. Proportionally, their influence was profound. Into the soul of Judaism they breathed renewed faith in the soil and renewed sense of the dignity of labor. Their heroic efforts achieved no real degree of financial success. Their tenacious settlement indicated, however, that what was needed was not mere patronage and subsidy, or cheap Arab labor, but more of what *Bilu* preached: more work, more self-dedication to the rebirth of the land by those who were willing to work it. Nonetheless, help was needed. From whom? No single individual or small society would suffice. Only help from Jews all over the world would do! An all-embracing movement was still lacking.

Suddenly, at this time, the settlers realized how unnaturally the land was being developed. The influx of funds for land purchase through PICA, the Palestine Jewish Colonial Society (later, Rothschild placed the administration of his privately financed settlements in

PICA hands), resulted in a land boom and in inflated prices in Jaffa. There was a sudden collapse. The Grand Porte in Constantinople became alarmed and ordered all sales of land to Jews to cease. For a while all further development in the *Yishuv* (Palestine Settlement) ceased.

Then controversy rent and splintered the direction-less Zionist movement. The zealous *Chovevei Zion* had no leadership or practical perspective. Millionaires, such as Rothschild and Baron de Hirsch, offered practical aid but no real enthusiasm for the creation of a nation. Theirs were well-intentioned real estate transactions, beneficent but without inspiration. Lack of leader-ship showed itself in pettiness of outlook. The move-ment had lost sight of its nobler purposes. The great Hebrew essayist, Ahad Ha'am, wrote searching ar-ticles from Russia calling for a selective, qualitative im-migration leading to a cultural rebirth rooted in the Hebrew language. His opponents demanded a gigantic mass immigration to the land, with little immediate re-gard for such luxuries as a cultural renaissance.

None of these programs sought negative ends. All held a purposeful, affirmative point of view. But lack of unity and organized, considered planning obstructed further progress.

In the midst of this crisis, Theodor Herzl brought or-der into chaos and set Zionists on the road to Israel. A Viennese journalist, Herzl had become the Paris cor-respondent for the distinguished newspaper, *Neue Freie Presse*. He was born in Budapest in 1860 of par-

ents who accepted assimilation as a virtue. For a year
after he received his degree of Doctor of Laws, Herzl
practiced law in Vienna. Then he turned to journalism
and playwriting and won sparkling success. A witty,
suave sophisticate with little interest in ritual, Herzl's
concern for Jewish affairs and for Judaism was, for the
first thirty-five years of his life, very limited.

In Paris, in 1894, Herzl's veneer of indifference was
shattered. While reporting the infamous Dreyfus affair,
the virulence of anti-Semitism overwhelmed him. After
intense spiritual trial, he wrote *Der Judenstaat* (*The
Jewish State*), published in 1896. In this book he expounded his plan for the redemption of the Jews. His
idea was that only in their own land could the Jews of
the world find their spiritual and physical salvation.

With burning energy, Herzl went to work. He lived
only eight years after the publication of his book; they
were by any yardstick eight of the most restless years
any man ever lived on this earth. Within one year following the publication of *Der Judenstaat*, he accomplished what none of his predecessors had been able to
achieve. He gathered together representatives of Jewry
from all over the world in a great assembly. The First
Zionist Congress was held in Basle, Switzerland, in August of 1897. A tall, handsome man with a long, black,
patriarchal beard, Herzl looked very much the prophet.
The hall thundered with cheers when he appeared. He
spoke deftly, with an assurance that was infectious. The
aim of Zionism, he proclaimed, was to establish a
home for the Jewish people, "publicly recognized,

legally secured." The Congress adopted an anthem, *Hatikvah* ("Hope") and a flag. Today, both anthem and flag are the emblems of the state of Israel.

Herzl's speech electrified the two hundred delegates. He spoke boldly as no Jew in memory had spoken. He did not beg for a piece of real estate, a refuge on sufferance, but a genuine homeland, free, unfettered, self-governed.

"At that Congress," wrote Herzl in his memoirs, "I founded the Jewish state."

A charter was Herzl's obsession. In the next seven years he crisscrossed Europe a dozen times in an effort to get it. He demanded, begged and cajoled audiences with the Sultan of Turkey, who controlled Palestine, with the Kaiser, with the Russian nobility, the Pope, the King of Italy and the British Foreign Office. He implored Rothschild to give up his sporadic efforts and to place his great prestige and financial resources at the disposal of the Zionist program. Wherever he traveled he spoke as the prime minister of his people; in his own mind there was no doubt that they supported his ambitions for them. And they, in turn, greeted him as the prophet of his age, cheered him in the streets and followed his travels and his writings as though he were, if not the Messiah, at least the harbinger of a messianic era.

In some circles, however, Herzl found bitter opposition. A thinker such as Ahad Ha'am was openly hostile and considered Herzl a parvenu or a naïve political zealot who was "rushing the Messiah." When Ahad

Ha'am and others were told that Herzl, on his own initiative, had promised the corrupt Sultan ten million
dollars of Jewish money in return for a charter, they
were aghast at his quixotic audacity. Herzl insisted to his
dying day that had he been able to deliver the ransom,
he himself could have brought a Jewish state to his people. For brief moments his failures and the bitterness of
the opposition discouraged him. And then his astonish-
ing spirit would surge forward. It was like, he said, toss-
ing a "red hot metal into cold water. Of course, if this
metal happens to be iron, it comes out steel."

By the Fifth Congress in 1901, Herzl had succeeded
in establishing a Jewish Colonial Trust, a bank to carry
out financial transactions for the movement, and a Jewish National Fund to purchase land. The Fund was to
stipulate that none of the lands leased to the settlers
could ever be used for resale and profit. When negotiations with the Sultan finally collapsed, Herzl, recognizing that the dissolution of the Turkish empire was at
hand, began to negotiate earnestly with the British government, then headed by Arthur James Balfour, who
later issued the famous Declaration of 1917.

Despite his commitments to journalism, to negotiations with many governments, and to the administration of the Zionist movement, Herzl found time to
write *Altneuland* in which he envisioned his dream
come true: Palestine settled and governed by Jews in a
free, democratic, cooperative commonwealth. The practical detail of his dream reveals the genius of man. Others hesitated even to hope; Herzl not only dreamed, but

"Greet all Palestine for me. Tell them I have given my heart's blood for my people."

Ten thousand people walked behind his plain pine coffin in Vienna, and wept as the great Jew of his era was laid to rest.

It is doubtful that Theodor Herzl considered his work successful. The vast horizon of his vision demanded a comparable range of accomplishment; it was almost too much to expect of one human being in one lifetime. But after his death the movement felt both a dreadful void and also the fulness of his achievement. He had begun amid chaos. He had established the goal: a free land in Palestine for all Jews who wished to live there. He had outlined the method to achieve it: a legally secured charter. Unswerving in his goal and confident in his means of reaching it, he had served undeterred the ideal of Zion.

As Herzl had judged, Turkish strength was ebbing. The British would hold the key to the coming struggle. Herzl's negotiations with the Balfour government had already prepared the ground for British-Zionist cooperation. Fortunately, others were ready to carry on his work.

The tide of immigration swept forward, and not only because of Zionist inspiration. The anti-Semitic uprisings in Kishineff, Russia, in 1903 sent frightened Russian Jews in search of safety in Palestine. Between 1904 and 1918 (the dates usually associated with the Second *aliyah*), more than 30,000 immigrants settled in Palestine.

dreamed accurately! The State of Israel bears remarkable resemblance to Herzl's *Altneuland*.

The horrible pogroms in Russia in 1903 profoundly disturbed Herzl and his followers. How could they wait patiently to plan and to build in meticulous detail while their brothers were being slaughtered in Russia? After a series of talks, Herzl received from Joseph Chamberlain, Colonial Secretary in the Balfour cabinet, tentative assurance that Britain would be willing to give the Jews a haven in Uganda, British East Africa. Herzl's considerations were twofold: if he could get a charter in the name of the Jewish people for Uganda, that would establish a precedent for a later charter in Palestine when, as he fully expected, the British inherited the Turkish territory. Second, the territory might immediately save imperiled lives. What, at the moment, could be more decisive?

At the Sixth Congress, Herzl presented the Uganda proposition to the delegates. Acrimonious debate showed his error, for the bitterest opponents were the Russian Jews who had suffered the most. Even Herzl, the great visionary of his people, had not realized how sacred was the memory of that special place—Palestine. The plan was rejected.

This bitter rebuff pained Herzl deeply. Worse than that, however, was the condition of his heart which, in the past few years, had grown ominously weaker. He forced himself to take a short rest, but it availed little. On July 3, 1904, his gallant heart throbbed its last beat. His last words to a friend at his bedside pleaded:

These were the more forward-looking emigrants from the Russian and Polish ghettos. They had decided that Russia held no future for them. In their practical idealism, they recognized that Palestine held no golden promises of material prosperity, but that they never expected. Their great objective was a cooperative commonwealth. Inspired by that ideal, they proved its practicability. Some of Israel's great leaders came with that *aliyah*, men like David Ben Gurion, Israel's first premier, and Yitzhak Ben Zvi, the second president.

These pioneers offered a sharp contrast to the widespread image of the European Jew bent and broken, concerned with petty dialectics. They walked erect and exalted the virtue of physical strength and courageous action. They took no nonsense from marauders and almost as little from the corrupt Turkish police. When reason and patience failed, they struck back forcefully, blow for blow. This *aliyah* accomplished much: it built farm colonies and reinforced them with disciplined defense units. Many of these same Jews had picked up a club against Russian Cossacks or Polish hoaligans; they were not prepared to endure once again that misery which had impelled them to settle in Palestine. Moreover, they were secure in their conviction that this land was theirs, legally and morally.

The *shomrim* (guards) brought together pioneers who were hand-picked for their bravery, for their skill in combat, and for their devotion to the cause of militant self-defense. They became the minute men, the militia of the Second Wave. Stories of their heroic exploits re-

sound in Israel's history like those American frontiers-
men in our own country.

In 1909, the Turkish Sultan was overthrown by the
new party of "Young Turks" who promised an era of
progress. New hopes for a charter stirred the Zionists,
but after a short time they discovered that the dreary
anachronism of the Sultan with his harems and the me-
dieval greed of his courtiers had been replaced by an
up-to-date despotism.

The Young Turks promised the national groups
within their empire—Serbs, Greeks, Kurds, Arabs and
Jews—some measure of autonomy. But the voice was
the voice of freedom, and the hand the heavy hand of
oppression. The charter seemed ever more distant. The
policy of Herzl's closest followers of devoting all ener-
gies to securing a political guarantee lost the support of
the Ninth Zionist Congress. The "practicals"—those
who demanded continued settlement and immigration
with or without a charter—carried the day. The defeat
of the Turks in the Balkan War of 1912 did not alter
the Young Turks' hostility to Zionist aims. Tenaciously
they clung to their waning empire.

About this time Chaim Weizmann, a Jewish chemist
who had left the Russian ghetto to settle in England,
became a dominant leader in the Zionist movement.
During the bitter Uganda debates, Weizmann, then
twenty-five, had opposed Herzl. He held that Zionists
had to build not only a physical haven in Palestine, but
also a world center for the Jewish spirit. In this way, the
Jews of the whole world could participate in and benefit

from the rebirth. It was the destiny of this brilliant scientist to achieve at least Herzl's goal of a charter by means of his immense prestige with British leaders.

When World War I broke out there were almost 100,000 Jews in Palestine. As yet, however, the *Yishuv* was not a self-supporting community. The war had consumed what little surplus it possessed. Export markets for its oranges and wines were severed. The Turks aggravated the difficulties of the settlers. Suspicious of the Jews whom they felt instinctively to be sympathetic to the Allied cause, the Turks set out to destroy the community. They forced the Land Trust and banks to close, and banned the many institutions dependent upon foreign support. Then they deported those who refused to serve in the Turkish army. A wave of terror engulfed the *Yishuv*. The Turks hanged those suspected of spying for the British. Systematic arrests, beating and torture of countless others followed. Epidemics deepened the misery of the land. Typhus and cholera, unchecked because of the pitiful shortage of physicians and medical supplies, ravaged the settlers. Then locusts swarmed over the countryside, reducing the field crops to shriveled bare stalks. The Jewish population shrank from 100,000 to only 55,000.

When the British, under General Allenby, invaded the country from Egypt, the land was divided for a whole year. Many starved while they waited for liberation.

Despite their suffering the Jews did not hesitate to fight. The war to end wars, to make the world safe for democracy, captured the heart of the inspired community. Under the banner of Vladimir Jabotinsky, a fiery Russian journalist, a Jewish Legion, recruited from Jews who stole across the Turkish lines, was formed in Alexandria. As the Zionist Mule Corps, the Legion diligently carried supplies to the British at Gallipoli. Later they helped purge Palestine of Turkish armies. Here were two bitterly ironic paradoxes: the Jews of Palestine joined forces with the Allies, and therefore stood alongside Russia, which for over a generation had persecuted Jews and continued to do so throughout the war. Secondly, Jewish military effort helped to liberate the Holy Land from the Turks not only for the Jews, but also for the Arabs of Palestine, Iraq and Syria. Throughout the war, the Arabs had avoided active participation in combat. Not long after the war, they were to proclaim with injured pride that the land and its sovereignty were theirs, earned by their simple presence on it. And it was they whom the British were to appear to prefer to their wartime comrades-in-arms, the Jews.

The Zionist movement in America began to mature during this period. The majority of American Jews had displayed little interest in Zionist aspirations. For most of them, their adopted land was *the* promised land. Never in the history of the Diaspora had any country treated Jews with such kindness and offered them such freedom and opportunity as had this blessed new land. It was only under the vigorous leadership of one of America's great men, Supreme Court Justice Louis D. Brandeis, that American Jewry united in the cause of

Zion. To accomplish this Brandeis employed the exquisite logic and elegance of his brilliant legal mind. He pointed out to Jews who feared that interest in Palestine might cast doubt upon their American patriotism the difference between a nationality and a nation.

Different nationalities exist within one nation quite properly, he said. Vigorously, and with great authority, he proclaimed: "Let no American imagine that Zionism is inconsistent with patriotism. Multiple loyalties are objectionable only if they are inconsistent. . . . The Jewish spirit . . . is essentially modern and essentially American. . . . Every American Jew who aids in advancing the Jewish settlement in Palestine, though he feels that neither he nor his descendants will ever live there, will likewise be a better man and a better American for doing so."

Brandeis stirred the American Jewish community to action; by 1917, $16 million had been collected for the relief of Jews, Christians and Moslems in Palestine. Food ships and medical units equipped by Hadassah, the women's arm of the Zionist movement, entered the port of Jaffa, and their precious cargos were distributed among all who needed help.

Thus the decimated community of Palestine struggled through the war, sustained only by the promise of the future: their land was to be ruled by a democratic power. This promise held new hope for the discouraged settlers.

## 3  THE PROMISE IS FULFILLED

Even after the close of the war the *Yishuv* continued to endure severe hardships. Ignoring their obvious self-interest, the Jews of Palestine had not sided with the Turkish occupying power, which would certainly have rewarded them in victory. Instead of taking the easier course, they had decided to join the forces of democracy which at first appeared doomed to defeat. True to their convictions, they could have made no other choice. They accepted at their face value the Allied slogans of a war for democracy, a war to end all war, which promised early fulfilment of their highest hope—the establishment of a free homeland for a peace-loving people.

In his Manchester laboratory, Chaim Weizmann had

devised a new method to produce large-scale quantities of acetone, a chemical essential to the manufacture of vitally needed TNT. As spokesman for a grateful nation, Lloyd George, then chairman of the War Munitions Committee, asked the scientist how Britain might reward him. Weizmann, it is said, answered with fitting humility: "I ask nothing for myself. All I ask is that you do something for my people."

Through the great prestige he enjoyed in his adopted homeland, Weizmann secured the support of many influential citizens and pursued the goal of winning a formal and official commitment from the British government in favor of the establishment of a Jewish homeland. Across the Atlantic in the United States, Louis Brandeis, powerfully assisted by Dr. Stephen S. Wise and Professor Richard Gottheil, urged President Wilson to use his best endeavors on behalf of the Zionist cause. Wilson, deeply moved by the spiritual appeal of Zionism, gave his assent and dispatched a message to Lloyd George, who had now become Prime Minister, pledging American support for a British statement of sympathy for the establishment of a Jewish homeland. As a result of these efforts, the Balfour Declaration was published by the British government on November 2, 1917. The Declaration was actually in the form of a letter addressed to Lord (Lionel Walter) Rothschild, a recent but devoted convert to Zionism, by Lord Balfour, Secretary of State for Foreign Affairs. For British Commonwealth leaders like Winston Churchill, Jan Smuts, Robert Cecil, Lloyd George, and Balfour himself, the

Declaration represented a wholehearted British commitment to Jewish statehood. The text of the Declaration reads as follows:

> I have much pleasure in conveying to you, on behalf of His Majesty's government, the following declaration of sympathy with Jewish Zionist aspirations, which has been submitted to and approved by the Cabinet:
>
> His Majesty's Government view with favor the establishment in Palestine of a national home for the Jewish people, and will use their best endeavors to facilitate their achievement of this object, it being clearly understood that nothing shall be done which may prejudice the civil and religious rights of existing non-Jewish communities in Palestine, or the rights and political status enjoyed by Jews in any other country.
>
> I should be grateful if you would bring this declaration to the knowledge of the Zionist Federation.

At this juncture of history, Herzl, had he still lived, could have asked for no more. In his book *Altneuland*, he envisaged a nation of Jews under a form of democratic self-government which guaranteed political and cultural rights to all.

Woodrow Wilson, expressing the sentiments of the Allied world, said, "I am persuaded that the Allied nations with the fullest concurrence of our own government and people are agreed that in Palestine shall be laid the foundations of a Jewish commonwealth."

The Jews of the world were hardly inclined to search for any hidden nuance or ambiguity in the language of the Balfour Declaration. A wave of optimism swept over the whole of world Jewry. Synagogues all over the world joyfully offered thanks to God for the goodness of His Providence.

A realistic view of the Near East might well have restrained the buoyancy of more hard-headed Zionists. The British, long accustomed to the policy of divide and rule, had also promised to sponsor an Arab kingdom for Emir Feisal, one of the sons of Hussein, Sherif of Mecca. Many of the British officials stationed in the Holy Land never wholly approved of the Jewish settlers, whose sturdy independence of mind was foreign to their colonial training. Unlike "Arab natives" whose sycophancy flattered "superior" whites, the Jews were not "natives" at all, but a free people in its own land. Accordingly, when Arab mobs, roused by agitators, rioted against Jewish settlements, British officers not infrequently stood aside and ignored the rioters. With few exceptions, the British military leaders never recognized or took seriously the meaning of the Balfour Declaration.

However, in 1922 the provisions of the Declaration were fully legalized, when a League of Nations Mandate gave Britain the responsibility, which finally ended in 1948, for administering the territory.

The Mandate was a challege to the Jews to show their mettle. The land needed people, services, and development. The response to the challenge was the third *aliyah*. The new immigrants carried in their hearts a mixture of disillusionment and vigorous hope. Their future in postwar Germany, Poland, Rumania (Russia

was excluded; the Bolsheviks treated Zionists as enemies
and forbade them to emigrate) seemed hopeless. Middle class life had disintegrated; Europe had grown old,
careworn, and melancholy. Palestine, under the Mandate, now promised a future of creative living. Between
1919 and 1923 the immigrants of the Third Wave restored the Jewish community of the country to its pre-
war population of 100,000. More important, they
brought a spirit of *halutziut*, of pioneering. In some re-
spects they had come at a most difficult time. With the
coming of the Mandate, the world Zionist movement
was expected to provide large sums of money for the
purchase and settlement of land. But in the wake of ex-
ultation over the establishment of the mandate and its
approval by the League of Nations came profound de-
jection. A number of non-Zionists who had given some
support in the past now believed that the international
Zionist organization should end its activities and let
the new territory fend for itself. As for the dues-paying
members of the Zionist movement, they offered all they
had to give—generous hearts but limited means.

The *halutzim*, however, did not despair. They had
rejected the amenities of middle class life in favor of the
hardships of farming. With religious zeal they drained
the swampland purchased at exorbitant prices from
Arab landowners by the Jewish National Fund. Their
labor promised them two rewards: first, the eradication
of malaria and second, the transformation of drained
swamps into fertile farmland. One young Polish immigrant of this *aliyah* who toiled in a Jezreel Valley

swamp was asked how he managed to survive the work. With characteristic self-directed Jewish humor he replied, "In Poland I used to work cleaning out spittoons. And what is a swamp? A national spittoon, no? Except that this spittoon at least belongs to me."

Maurice Samuel relates in his moving book, *Harvest in the Desert*, the epigrammatic philosophy of the *Halutzim* who fed the cattle while they themselves went hungry. "After all," they said wryly. "We are Zionists; they are not."

These painful trials and costly errors yielded at least the first beginnings of a new social and political order. A generation of bronzed, muscular youngsters grew up, forward-looking and unafraid. Well-organized committees began to aid new arrivals, placing them where they would serve themselves and the land most effectively. Careful planning and ordered direction quickened land development.

Suddenly all this fell apart. In 1925 a fourth *Aliyah* all but inundated the country. In one year 34,000 immigrants poured in from Poland, Rumania, Lithuania and Germany. The facilities for handling them collapsed. These immigrants entered the country without any real eagerness to begin a new life on the land, like the *Halutzim*. Many of them were petty merchants who hoped to invest their few zlotys in small business. The semiskilled laborers among them hoped to find employment in established industry. The land was not ready for them. As they spent their money in the cities for the necessities of life, inflation set in. A land boom mushroomed. Then in one nightmarish year the economy collapsed. Little soda and cigarette kiosks sprouted on Tel Aviv street corners during the 1925 Palestine depression, not unlike American apple stands in the early thirties. By 1927, there were 7,000 unemployed. In 1929, however, the economy began to recover. There were now 162,000 Jews in the country and all who wanted work could find it. The small "capitalists" whose funds had been lost went to work like ordinary people.

The country was beginning to come of age; medical science was rapidly eliminating malaria and trachoma, the scourges of the Near East; newly built hydroelectric works promised power for healthy economic expansion. Palestine's Arabs shared the progress of the new state; compared to the fellahin subjects of neighboring Arab monarchies, they enjoyed a genuine prosperity.

Until 1929, Arabs and Jews cooperated in constructive endeavors, and this actually was the rule during a period when the ratio of Arab to Jewish population was high—five to one—and the numbers of the British military and police garrisons low.

Then, apparently out of nowhere came sudden inflammatory rumors, charges that the Jews were attacking Arabs and desecrating the Mosque of Omar in Jerusalem. Before it could be made clear that the Mosque was untouched, religious riots broke out. Excitable extremists instigated by the infamous Mufti of Jerusalem (who later worked actively for Hitler during the last war) aroused the Arab population of Palestine, using pseudoreligious slogans where political incitements failed.

In the town of Hebron an Arab mob ran amuck and massacred sixty-five Jews, men, women and children. Not a gun for defense was to be found in the Jewish quarters. Other similar attacks followed. The British constabulary explained them away as local incidents. When it became obvious that the Mandatory government could not protect them, the settlers organized in self-defense. Following these Arab riots of 1929, peaceful relations between Jews, Arabs and the British never prevailed for any extended period.

If the purpose of the riots was to intimidate the Jews and drive them out of the country, the census records indicate total failure. The Fifth Aliyah began soon after, in 1932, made up of refugees from the gathering storm of Nazism in Central Europe. By 1935, 375,000 Jews had settled in Palestine. Legally or illegally, they came back to the land of their fathers.

During these years, Arab opposition to Jewish settlement became steadily more intransigent, despite Arab control of vast lands with room for scores of millions of people. Not one of the feudal monarchs who controlled these vast territories had ever proposed so much as a simple plan for revitalizing their long-abused lands. On the contrary, these monarchs preferred to rule in callous disregard for their subjects' welfare. Palestine was a threat to this kind of rule. Arab progress there might stimulate dissatisfaction among the Near East's exploited, disease-ridden masses. The very existence of such a prosperous democratic state threatened the social and economic foundations of the decadent Arab kingdoms; therefore Jewish settlement had to be curbed and destroyed. Cynically, the rulers harnessed nascent Arab nationalism to their own selfish ends.

Even before the first riots, in 1920, the British had set aside lands across the Jordan for a kingdom for Emir Abdullah, to counterbalance the power of Ibn Saud in Arabia. All that these two despots shared in common was hatred of each other. The British, bound to the antiquated system of divide and rule, were dividing badly and ruling worse.

The short-lived labor government of Ramsay Mac-Donald in 1924 continued this policy. Again in 1929, when Labor resumed office, Lord Passfield, Colonial Secretary, who as Sidney Webb had written a glowing eulogy of Soviet Communism, adopted a report recommending that Jewish immigration into Palestine be limited to an additional 20,000 settlers. This policy was incorporated in the British White Paper of 1930, which imposed crippling restrictions on Jewish land purchase and development.

Weary with disappointment because of loss of faith in the nation which he had trusted, Chaim Weizmann resigned as leader of World Zionism.

Encouraged by the growth of Nazi power in Europe, the Mufti launched a new wave of disturbances in 1936. The official Palestine government's response to Arab attacks was to disarm Jews and jail their leaders for attemping to defend themselves. These were years to try the souls of saints. The *Yishuv* vowed to defend itself but not to engage in retaliations. *Havlagah* (self-restraint) became the slogan of the settlers.

The riots continued and the British sent commissions to investigate the situation. Lord Peel reported in 1937 that there was no reason to assume that Jewish settlement in Palestine had retarded Arab development. He found that Arabs were living far better in Palestine than anywhere else; their health conditions were infinitely superior. Their population had doubled in twenty years. Their life expectancy was the highest in the whole Arab world. The riots, he suggested, were fomented by political agitators for their own sinister purposes.

Continued Arab hostility led to the White Paper of 1939, which limited immigration to 15,000 a year for five years after which it was to stop completely unless the Arabs agreed to further Jewish immigration. This latest discriminatory White Paper completely repudiated the spirit of the Balfour Declaration. It was the harshest blow that the *Yishuv* had yet suffered. It can only be understood in the light of Neville Chamberlain's policy of appeasing Hitler, Mussolini and their Arab ally, the Mufti.

Soon afterward there followed the horror of the floating coffins. Jews, fleeing from the tortures of the concentration camps and the crematoria of Hitler, packed themselves in the filthy holds of tramp steamers, oversized tugboats, anything their friends abroad could beg or buy, and set sail for freedom in Palestine. These pitiful craft were intercepted by British naval vessels and forced back to their point of origin in Hitler's Europe. Protesting, the refugees were dragged from the holds, then interned in detention camps.

The *Yishuv* did not sit idly by. Openly and with pride the Jews of Palestine fought back. In the dead of night human floating chains assisted refugees from the boats to land. Despite official threats and punishment, *Haganah* (Defense), an effective underground army, formed its ranks to fight for survival.

The Arab leaders whom Britain had appeased in turn betrayed their appeasers, and openly sided with the Axis powers. Hitler and Mussolini enjoyed the support of the leader of Palestine's Arabs, the Mufti. When the Palestine Regiment was formed, nine-tenths of its ranks were made up of Jews. More than half of the Arab contingent deserted or joined the Axis armies. The Regiment later became the nucleus of the Jewish Brigade.

David Ben Gurion, the white-maned leader of Palestine's Jews, expressed the spirit of the settlers: "We shall fight the war as if there were no White Paper. And we shall fight the White Paper as if there were no war."

The Jewish Brigade fought heroically in the Near East and in North Africa. At Tobruk, the first soldier to fall for the British cause was a Jew, a refugee who had escaped from Czechoslavakia only to be dragged off a rescue ship and interned in a detention camp. Nevertheless, he had volunteered for desert duty. He fought, not for British colonialism, but against Hitler's barbarism, and for a free Palestine.

Throughout the war, the battle of immigration continued. Tension mounted after the end of hostilities. When troops leveled a settlement at Birya as an act of reprisal, three thousand settlers, defended by Haganah units, returned in the dead of night and rebuilt it before daylight.

The British Government's harsh and unsympathetic policy sorely tried the patience of the *Yishuv*. Small activist groups, scornful of *Haganah's* non-retaliation program, were formed to fight terror with terror. They remained a minority; their own people would never accept a religion of violence and the terrorist assassination of Lord Moyne was condemned on all sides. Organizations like the *Irgun Zvai Leumi* and the Stern group never found mass support among the people. Soon after the establishment of the State, the government ordered them to disband.

In July of 1945, the Conservative government was replaced by the Labor Party. The new government through its Foreign Minister, Ernest Bevin, continued previous repressive policies in Palestine. President Truman urged that the gates of Palestine be opened to the surviving remnant of the Nazi concentration camps. Bevin coldly answered, "if you want them there, take them yourself." His intensified blockade against refugee ships evoked great bitterness in the *Yishuv*. Bankrupt of policy, the British announced their abandonment of the Mandate and withdrawal from Palestine. The General Assembly of the United Nations took up the problem.

Working against time (the Mandate was due to end

in May, 1948), the British began a two-year campaign
to hamper the development of the Jewish state. This
was the eleventh hour bid of a declining power to retain
a vestige of authority through its own instrument, the
Arab League, and thereby to retain what could be saved
from its debacle in the Near East. In subsequent years
the political unreality of the plan became clear. Egypt
forced the British out of Suez and undermined its position in the Sudan. Turbulent Iran expropriated British
oil properties. The Arab League itself proved wholly in-
effectual and was torn apart by bitter internal feuds.

During 1946-48, the terror reached its peak in Palestine. The government jailed 2,700 people including the
elected leaders of the *Yishuv*. In an attempt to blockade
the Jews from outside aid, the Jewish Agency was attacked. Demands on the community to surrender its
arms were rejected. In reprisal, captured Jewish soldiers
were flogged to intimidate the rebellious *Yishuv*. The
extremists retaliated by flogging British soldiers. A
corrosive, dreadful battle of wills continued.

Finally, on November 29, 1947, the United Nations
General Assembly voted a Palestine partition plan to establish independent Jewish and Arab states in the
mandated area. The Jewish case had been brilliantly
presented before the United Nations by the American
Zionist leader, Rabbi Abba Hillel Silver, thus marking
the full maturity of the political leadership of the
world's largest Jewish community. The British closed
the Haifa refinery, jeopardizing the country's fuel supply. To halt the trade of the territory, they froze Pales-

tine assets in British banks. The Arab Legion, under British officers, openly prepared to attack the Jews after withdrawal. If the Israelis proclaimed their independence, the Legion would deal with them.

David Ben Gurion and his small band of patriots stood firm. On the fifth day of *Iyar*, 5708, according to the Hebrew calendar, May 14, 1948, by the common calendar, the day when the Mandate was due to end, the provisional governing council proclaimed the establishment and independence of the State of Israel. Within the hour in the United States, President Truman announced America's *de facto* recognition of the new government of Israel.

Two days later the Council elected Chaim Weizmann the first President of the nation.

The world's newest nation could afford no time to rejoice at its independence. Next morning the armies of six Arab nations attacked *en masse*. Azzam Pasha, Secretary General of the Arab League, indicated the mood of the aggressors: "This will be a war of extermination and a momentous massacre which will be spoken of like the Mongol massacres."

At first glance the Pasha's fierce words seemed hardly an idle boast. The Arab nations could recruit soldiers from a population of 35,000,000. The Jewish enemy, with the sea at their backs, consisted of only 650,000 combat-weary people.

Egypt began by bombing Tel Aviv, while Syrian and Lebanese units marched south. The (Transjordan) Arab Legion moved toward Jerusalem. Iraqi armies swept westward. The *Haganah*, hitherto an underground defense force which had to rely on homemade weapons and ammunition, came out into the open to meet well-equipped Arab armies.

Settlers in the frontier outposts took shelter in underground bunkers. Heavy artillery blasted away their homes; the enemy slaughtered their livestock and fired their grain. At night the beleaguered settlers crept out of hiding and by a series of dazzling and heroic harassing maneuvers kept the invaders from moving rapidly against the key points of the country.

The Arab Legion bombarded the Jewish quarter in the old city of Jerusalem, and its age-old synagogues and holy places were blasted into rubble. Finally, surrender was arranged on May 28. Only thirty-nine defenders capable of bearing arms had survived. In the New City, 100,000 Jews, subjected to a merciless bombardment, were threatened with extinction if the lifeline to Tel Aviv were not maintained. In a daring operation, the Israeli Army hacked out its own ten-mile-long "Burma Road" through the wild hills south of Arab-held Latrun to Bab-el-Wad, which had remained in the control of the Jewish forces. The road saved the city from certain destruction and became known as the Road of Valor in tribute to the young boys and old men who built it.

A few hours before the first United Nations truce of June 11 came into force, Israeli bombers attacked Damascus, capital of Syria. On Independence Day, the Jewish state had owned not a single bomber. During the intervening weeks volunteers flew planes into the country from America, in defiance of British and American government embargos. The new state, armed and ready, began to hit back for victory.

The truce lasted a month. No one believed that it would be anything more than a breathing spell. A day and a half before the expiration of the truce, the Egyptians attacked in the Negev, the southernmost desert area of the country. Israeli commando squads moved in and around them and cut them to shreds. In ten days the Egyptians suffered 2,000 casualties. Meanwhile, in the central part of the country the Israeli units forced the Arab Legion back to Latrun. Tel Aviv was safe. In Jerusalem, newly arrived Israeli artillery returned shell for Arab shell, and thousands of Arabs fled from the Old City. In the North, Israeli columns captured Nazareth and put to flight an assorted army of Arabs, supported by German and British mercenaries. Galilee was secured.

The tide of the war had turned. Israel was prepared to storm besieged Jerusalem. The continued momentum of battle would have quickly cleared the country of its invaders. On July 18, however, another truce was imposed. The nation that had been created by the United Nations and had vowed to respect international law acquiesced.

It was an unreal truce, broken almost every day of its duration by the Arabs, especially the Egyptians. As the *King Farouk*, Egypt's flagship, reconnoitered in Israeli waters, small Israeli ships sank it. The Egyptians continued to harass the Negev, severing pipelines and polluting water supplies. In a daring two week campaign which ended in early January, 1949, the Israeli Army flushed the Egyptians out of the Negev and occupied defense positions across the border. Another truce was ordered. Against military advice, the Israeli government again complied.

The day the truce became effective, January 7, 1949, Israeli fighter planes shot down five Royal Air Force fighters that had trespassed over the battle zone for obscure purposes. An aroused British public demanded to know why its government had openly intervened. Even the British Foreign Office had to face the inevitable. By the end of the month the government of Britain had recognized the government of Israel.

For once history had done justice to the Jews. Warlike and well trained, the Arabs had held every advantage: ample arms, a voice in the council of nations, powerful friends, numbers and geography were on their side. The Jews had only the fervent support of their decimated people, their own courage, and the favor of a long-abiding and inscrutable Providence. After twenty centuries of terror, flight, and unspeakable oppression the Jews had stood, fought, and won.

# 4 THE LAND REBORN

All practical considerations should have led Zionist leaders to seek a more promising land on which to establish the Jewish state.

The land was sick and tired. It drowsed under shifting sands. Streams meandered aimlessly here and there, and precious water seeped into the ground and was lost. Sometimes the waters crept into foul lowlands, there to be bottled up in turgid pools of muck and slime. Above these pestilential swamps swarmed anopheles mosquitoes, infecting with malaria anyone who ventured near. The ancient hills, baked dry by the hot sun, had long ago lost any trace of life. In the South, the land was shrouded by desolate arid desert. On the sea coast, the

Mediterranean winds blew hot. Possessing neither trees nor foliage, the once-fertile coastal strip seemed still hotter. Crumbled terraces along the sloping hills testified mutely to a once-flourishing agriculture. The country lay solemn and still, like a vast graveyard. But it did evoke memories, especially poignant ones for those whose history gave them a claim to this sad, beloved land.

For its 8,000 square miles, a territory as large as New Jersey, Israel's topography is remarkably varied. The Jordan, the nation's only sizable river, begins high in the Syrian mountains, whose summits are hoary with eternal snow; for more than 150 miles its waters gouge through the hills, falling ever deeper until they enter the torrid cul-de-sac of the Dead Sea.

But neglect, not nature, had ravaged the land. Where now there were deserts and barren hillsides, there had once thrived productive farmlands. The sandy coastline had been famous in days of old for its magnificent groves. And even in its earliest days, the Galilean hills were famed grazing land and vineyards. Memories still live. Once this had been a land of milk and honey. The new settlers vowed that once again, this dry and barren land would bear fruit.

Before the creation of the modern Zionist movement, those Jews who came to Palestine avoided the land. In the cities they clustered about their synagogues. Supported mostly by funds from little coin boxes in synagogues all over the world, they kept alive faith in the return. During harvest time, fulfilling the Biblical command, they built the *Sukkah*, a fragile hut of branches, in gratitude for crops they had not sowed. They prayed and they sighed as they looked upon the land. And they waited. The more devout believed that the time was not yet ripe; the Messiah had yet to appear. The land slumbered quietly on.

The roots of Zionism lie deeply buried in the soil of national rebirth. The land was to be reborn through the labor of the people; the people would be redeemed by their labor on the land. Such an ideal represented not a simple return to the past but a plan for building the future on the foundation of the past.

The new Zionists, under Herzl, Max Nordau (who proclaimed that to be an assimilated Jew meant to be "an internal cripple"), Chaim Weizmann, and David Ben Gurion dared to map out such a future. They knew that the land would not be reborn by conventional means. Not through known and accepted means of paying one's money and taking one's choice of a few dunams of land, would Zion flourish. Were that the way, who would venture into the swamp? Who would settle the lonely outposts where unfriendly Bedouin roamed? Who would choose a stretch of desert, endure sandstorms and blazing heat to nurse a spare strand of grain, when a season's work might be engulfed in minutes by a dark cloud of locusts?

Direct subsidy fostered the earliest settlement. With no hope of profit, Baron Rothschild had patronized colonies, built huge wine cellars, and purchased at artificially inflated prices the surplus grape crops. In 1870

the Alliance Israélite Universelle, a French philanthropic organization, set up the Mikveh Israel agricultural school to stimulate interest in the land. But both
efforts sought limited ends. There was no pretense to
evoke the spiritual incentive needed to revitalize a nation. Dependent on kindly patrons, the colonists were
hardly prepared to carry on should funds be wanting.
When the great philanthropist Baron Maurice de
Hirsch purchased farm land in Argentina and financed
the transfer of Jews to work it, some, attracted by the
opportunity, forsook the struggling colonies in Palestine. In the foreign land a few fortunate entrepreneurs succeeded. With their efforts they built not a
home, but a private business. The less fortunate found
themselves destitute when the generous subsidy was
spent.

It became clear that the redemption of the land of
Israel could not come about unless the task were shared
in common by the whole people. Those working the
land must be considered no less than the pioneer troops
of the Jewish people.

Yet even the fiercely idealistic *Biluim* failed in the
task. They have been compared to the westward surging
pioneers in America. The comparison is not altogether
apt. The American pioneers could lay claim to free
lands and drew on the resources of a friendly government. The *Biluim* had to purchase every dunam of
land. The best areas were occupied or priced prohibi-
tively, and the government offered obstruction, not pro-
tection.

PICA, the Palestine Jewish Colonization Society, founded by Baron de Hirsch, purchased land for individuals, gave them rudimentary training in agriculture and sent each on his own way. Sometimes an individual succeeded. Those who failed resented the few who were successful for their use of hired labor and their upstart arrogance. They could certainly feel little kinship with affluent Jewish businessmen and farmers, who denied jobs to Jews and hired cheap Arab labor instead. This did little to foster national unity.

With the Third *aliyah* some idealists appeared whose love for the land was blended with a commitment to cooperative endeavor. These *halutzim* abhorred the standards of the farmer who profited from another's labor. Imbued with the spirit of democratic socialism, these artisans, intellectuals, and small merchants dedicated themselves to simple toil. They wished neither to exploit nor to be exploited. They sought only to contribute their energy and the profit of their labor to the cause of a resurgent, democratic land. Cooperative agricultural colonies were to fulfill this ideal. Sharing labor and profit, the cooperatives would never employ labor for profit.

The movement took strong hold after World War I when hopes for social democracy, evoked by wartime promises, soared in Europe. Life on the *kibbutz* (collective farm) was not comfortable; but it was also never purposeless. Everyone pitched in; both husband and wife worked in the fields or at other designated tasks. Their children were reared in a communal nursery;

everyone ate in the communal dining room; trading and cultural affairs were freely discussed and decisions democratically adopted. The *kibbutz* educated its own children; it provided its own food, even its own manu- factured goods. The goal was self-efficiency through labor.

In the early days, the old settlers laughed at the dreamers and PICA reluctantly advanced them land. But when the Jewish National Fund for the purchase of land was established, with its provision that no land acquired might ever be resold for personal profit, the *kibbutz* movement found security and general accept- ance.

No task was too arduous for the *halutzim*. When they heard that the famed land buyer, Joshua Hankin, who wandered about the countryside looking for land for the Fund, had come upon a barren desert patch or a thousand dunams of swampland, the *kibbutzim* would immediately send cadres to reclaim and plant the land. Their achievements raised the spirit of the entire *Yishuv* and set worthy standards for the community. A *kibbutz* member, viewing the desert sands, commented with characteristic bravado, "A desert—what is it but an un- cultivated farm." This bold attitude expressed the zeal of those who transformed barren soil into fertile land capable of bearing rich harvests.

Like each of the vital forces in the movement to re- build Palestine, the *kibbutzim* occupied a special place at a very special time. These small integrated collective institutions taught the lesson that redemption was the task and concern of all. There could be no place for personal aggrandizement in Zionism. The *kibbutzim* also taught by example that a fruitful life could be enjoyed upon the land. Hard work demanded no apology. When thousands of urban-bred immigrants poured into Israel after the coming of statehood, the *kibbutzim* above all showed that farming offered a bright and useful future.

Today the *kibbutzim* stand as a symbol of past pioneering days. There is little reason to believe that they will play as large a role in the future development of the land as they did in the past. New settlers have been reluctant to bind themselves within the stern discipline of collective living. Oriental Jews from Yemen and North Africa, as well as the newcomers from the great cities of Europe, cherish middle class standards. They believe that mothers ought to raise their own children in their own home. These newcomers are decidedly not *kibbutz*-minded.

The *kibbutzim* first initiated essential soil-testing. They were first also to carry out experiments to determine the physical capacity of the soil. Today, the Ministry of Agriculture is planning land exploitation through one comprehensive program. The wide variations in climate allow for great diversification of crops. Winter rains, for example, usually provide enough water for winter and spring crops. But the hot Mediterranean sun blisters the land in the summertime. Accordingly, surplus winter rains are being stored in especially constructed watersheds for use in irrigation, and in areas which never get enough rainfall. Almost 25 per cent of the cultivated land is now under irrigation; a few short years ago much of this was wasteland.

The government plans to achieve caloric self-sufficiency within a dozen years following the establishment of the state, at which time the population is expected to reach 2,000,000. Citrus, the most important of Israel's crops, is to provide the needed export surplus to purchase wheat, tea and coffee. In the desert and in the hill country, the ministry has planted more than 16,-000,000 trees during the last half dozen years. All were raised from shoots in Israel nurseries and will serve as windbreaks to conserve the soil during floods and droughts.

Not only has the face of the land changed but also the character of its livestock. Certain breeds of goats which consumed more than they produced are being systematically replaced by a less voracious variety, and also with sheep, which are much more productive. In the newly seeded pasturelands of the Negev and Galilee, successful experiments are being conducted in the practicability of herding beef cattle.

Industrial crops to help cut down imports are beginning to provide raw materials for manufactures. New varieties of flax and cotton are taking root in Israel soil. If the government's experiment with the Juncus plant is successful, the nation's new paper mills will gain a valuable raw material. A variety of sugar beets for reducing both raw sugar and raw alcohol has been found; by 1960 Israel should have all the sugar it needs for domestic use. From the ubiquitous sunflower, from groundnut, from flax and sesame previous edible oils are being extracted. Tobacco has yielded so successfully that it has become an export. Besides citrus crops, the climate of Israel's hill country and the subtropical lowlands make possible a thriving fruit industry. Abundant grape harvests will soon lead to profitable wine exports. Already 3,000 acres of bananas are under cultivation. Avocado pears, a luxury cash crop, may soon provide a valuable export commodity to supplement exports of honey, olive oil and dates.

Scientific Israel farmers use modern threshers, electric milkers and tractors. Of the nation's 180,000 Arabs, about 150,000 live on some 15,000 Arab-owned farms. Until recently, those farms were operated with the most ancient methods. A tractor was an object of mystery. Techniques of crop rotation, terracing and soil conservation rarely benefited the Arab agricultural economy. Today, government agricultural agents introduce scientific methods to Arab farmers and tractors driven and maintained by Arab peasants are now a familiar feature of the Arab landscape.

At the turn of the century twenty-two settlements were struggling for survival. Five thousand Jews, out of a total Jewish population of 70,000 lived on the land. By 1948 the population had increased to 700,000; more than one quarter lived on the land; approximately 175,-000 in three hundred settlements. Then in 1948 came statehood and a flood of newcomers—the old, the infirm, the disconsolate, the miserable remnants of Hitler's Europe. It was not easy to convince these urban refugees to make their future on the land. But the government outlined a goal drawn from the spirit of the past and applicable at all times: rebuild your own land and in so doing rebuild your own lives. The immigrants understood and responded. More than a fifth of them took up labor on the soil. In 1955 Israel's population numbered 1,750,000 of whom 330,000 made their homes on the land.

The prosaic facts of Israel's agriculture—new crops, self-sufficiency, soil reclamation—should not obscure the romance of the achievement they represent. Here was a people driven from the land, prevented by law from working the soil, forced to live in cramped and unnatural ghettos. Here was a land, despoiled and barren, for centuries untouched by loving hands, cynically exploited, together with its inhabitants, by many conquerors. United, the people, used to urban comfort, and the land, unused to plow or scythe, redeemed one another. The people poured out their sweat in toil, the land evoked memory and hope, and in time old wastes yielded new harvests and the soul of a tired people found new strength and life.

# 5 A LANGUAGE LIVES AGAIN

In the early days of its development, the *Yishuv* (Jewish settlement in Palestine) struggled not for well-being but simply for being itself. A piece of land, an untroubled night, a few pounds to buy a plow or a sackful of seed, a charter to legalize a settlement—these modest ambitions filled the minds of the settlers. Conscious cultural creativity was a luxury yet to be enjoyed: for the moment, the land had to be restored and the people regenerated through the act of restoring their ancient soil.

Yet at no time was the Zionist cause without its proponents of the need for a Hebrew cultural renaissance as an indispensable part of the rebirth of land and peo-

ple. There had been for two millennia a people without
a land, and a land without a people: now, in this new
century, the two were to become one. This was a consecrated act to be achieved within the framework of an
ancient culture and tradition. Thus, as early in modern
times as the Fifth Zionist Congress in 1901, Ahad
Ha'am and the small band of "Lovers of Zion" took
sharp issue with Herzl for his apparent indifference to
cultural revival. They recognized Herzl's lack of Jewish
identification in his early years, and understood that his
so-called "practicality" stemmed from this.

To such men as Ahad Ha'am, the essayist, Chaim
Nachman Bialik, the poet, and Eliezer ben Yehudah, the
dedicated philologist, Palestine had to evolve not just
as a haven for Jews, but as a center for the development
of the Jewish Spirit. Weizmann, who inherited world
Zionist leadership from the so-called "politicals" during
the years when the movement was maturing, reflected
the views of the "culturalists" and understood their
practical importance for the rebirth of the state.

A new culture, these partisans maintained, could
evolve only through the rebirth of the ancient language,
Hebrew. The practical difficulties were enormous.
Throughout the entire world there were relatively few
Jews who could speak Hebrew. For the great majority
of Jews Hebrew was the language of synagogue, prayer,
and of rabbinical scholarship. Recognizing the difficulties, the culturalists stubbornly insisted that it was no
more unrealistic to assume that an inspired people
would learn to speak its historic language than that it

could revitalize its historic soil. Zionism demanded the loftiest in effort and aspiration: they reminded their opponents that to settle for anything less than the Hebrew language would represent a compromise which no good Zionist could accept without loss of self-respect. But more than that, a nation was unthinkable without its own language, without an idiom characteristically its own, evocative of the color and grace of its people.

But how were a few academicians to introduce and modernize a tongue for the everyday use of a nation unfamiliar with it?

Until World War I, settlers in the Yishuv spoke an assortment of tongues, among them Russian, German, French and English, the languages of the various places of Jewish dispersal. Only a spirited minority spoke Hebrew. Linguistically, a common denominator for many was Yiddish, the tongue spoken by Jews throughout central and eastern Europe. But though expressively warm and intimate, Yiddish was to the culturalists a reflection of the tragedy of Exile. For them, it was stamped with the stigma of the ghetto. It was the language of defeat and humiliation.

Obviously, the first place to re-establish the use of Hebrew was in the schools. Once it became the language of the children at school and at play, it would become the language of the land within a generation. The schools, however, were administered by philanthropic organizations which sponsored them; the language taught was that of the country from which the funds flowed. Thus, the schools operated by the Alliance Is-

raélite Universelle taught French. Its financial support-
ers, with headquarters in Paris, thought in French, so,
they wondered, why not French for Palestine? The
British who financed an Evelina de Rothschild school
utilized English as the language of instruction. The
Hilfsverein der Deutschen Juden, a German-Jewish organization, insisted upon German as *the* language and
that nothing else would do.

In this Babel of tongues, one tongue had to supplant
all others. This was the problem to be solved.

However, it should not be thought that Hebrew education was completely neglected. Many schools in the
*Yishuv,* including the important Herzliah High School,
the first Jewish secondary school in Palestine, taught
in Hebrew. But many a student at a Hebrew-speaking
school might well find his family's faces blank were he
to use the Hebrew language at home. It was more likely
that on the streets among his own playmates he would
have a better chance of getting some response.

Maurice Samuel tells a story of the two Hebraists,
Bialik and Ahad Ha'am, walking along a street in Tel
Aviv and unhappily discussing the meager progress the
language had made toward becoming the country's ver-
nacular. Ahad Ha'am spotted a young boy passing by
and pulled his ear without warning. The boy jumped
and cried out, *"Hamor Zaken!"* Literally translated
from Hebrew the phrase means, "You old donkey!"
The old man took the insult with a smile, turned beam-
ing to Bialik and said, "You see, we need more of *that!"*

Strangely enough, those who most fervently worked

for a rebirth of Hebrew were not those who lived with it every day of their lives—the strictly religious groups—who considered use of the holy tongue for secular purposes to be blasphemy. Hebrew was the language of prayer and study, not, as it once had been, of the marketplace and the field. To make it mundane and utilitarian was to demean it, in their opinion.

The champions of the language had themselves been reared in the homely comfort of Yiddish and their own national tongues, and they had to struggle hard to master Hebrew. They spoke Yiddish or German or Russian because these languages were native to them. Only out of a sense of dedication did they write plays, poems, and essays in Hebrew. In our own day, it would be not unlike some Ernest Hemingway, against all his native instinct, writing his novels in a newly revived Anglo-Saxon idiom.

Entirely on his own, Eliezer ben Yehudah worked feverishly to complete his many-volumed *General Dictionary of the Hebrew Language*, in which he constructed new words from old generic roots. His task was as complex in execution as it was vast in scope. In his dictionary, which was to be the definitive lexicon of living Hebrew, Ben Yehudah included words describing objects not even dreamed of in Biblical times. He included those words which would enable a Hebrew-speaking child or adult to say "zipper," "baseball," "airplane" or "howitzer." He had to discover words for "electricity," "train," "automobile." In a short space of years he had to create what normally takes a people many generations to evolve. But Ben Yehudah was almost fanatical in his dedication to the task before him. In his own home in Jerusalem he insisted that not a word other than Hebrew be heard, and he would refuse to answer questions asked in any other tongue. As a result of this single-minded devotion to the cause of language, his family was ridiculed by neighbors who used Hebrew in the synagogue on the Sabbath, then stored it away for the next holy day.

Enthusiasts like Ben Yehudah and his family disciplined themselves to use Hebrew throughout the week but others could manage only a few hours a day. In public places for appearance's sake, in their writings for posterity, and as a matter of principle, the Hebraists struggled bravely with the language; in their own homes they unburdened themselves of the severe, unfamiliar tongue, and relaxed with Yiddish. The Hebraists were as much pioneers in the battle for a rebirth of culture as were the halutzim in the campaign for the regeneration of the soil. That the *Yishuv* as a whole did not immediately follow their path indicated only that Zionism —the total idea—had yet to come of age.

The internal struggle between the languages rumbled on until before the beginnings of World War I. A climax was soon to develop which would provide a test case.

By 1913, the country's intellectuals had been completely won over to Hebrew. Educators had oriented their thinking to the problems of Hebrew pedagogy. The same year saw the beginning of construction of the

Haifa Technical Institute on Mount Carmel. Its benefactors were Jacob Schiff, the New York banker, and
the affluent Wissotsky family in Russia, and the German *Hilfsverein* sponsored the project. When the Zionist members of the Institute learned that the language
of instruction was to be German they resigned in a
body. The incident sent a tremor of discord vibrating
throughout the land and in Zionist circles around the
world. The *Hilfsverein* directors answered by dismiss-
ing the protestors. This drastic action evoked a happy
response. The teachers set up their own schools, financed by the Zionist movement. The system of Hebrew-speaking schools created by the nation-in-exile
had begun.

The vigorous reaction of the *Yishuv* overwhelmed the
*Hilfsverein* directors, who compromised with the Hebraists and allowed some subjects to be taught in Hebrew. The world war broke out the following year and
after that date the German language lost every vestige
of its former prestige. Nine years later, when the Mandate for Palestine was ratified by the League of Nations,
so deeply had Hebrew taken root that one of the Ar-
ticles of Mandate established Hebrew as one of the
three official languages of the territory, the others being
Arabic and English.

The Hebrew language served to unite the varied cultures of the *Yishuv*. One can hardly imagine Israel today without its national tongue. What would have been
the cultural consequence of its absence during those
hectic days immediately after independence in 1948?

Every hour, day and night, for three and a half years, an average of twenty-three immigrants poured into the land. They came from the detention camps of Cyprus, from Austria, Germany, Poland and Italy, from exotic communities in Tripoli, Libya, Yemen and Iraq, from Yugoslavia, from Aden and Turkey. This influx of 718,-ooo Jews came from sixty countries in all. In less than four years more than twice as many people entered Palestine as had been admitted during the thirty years of the Mandate.

All were Jews. But how many different kinds of Jews! What could long-robed Yemenites, from a hill country isolated in time and history, have in common with sophisticated French or German Jews? The memory was there—in the hearts of both—for the land and its Biblical promise. But these new citizens of Israel could not speak to one another. It was vital that all should learn the new-old tongue. Hebrew, it developed, had become Israel's most effective instrument in the struggle for national unity. All the languages of the Diaspora were welded into one: almost from the hour they landed in Haifa, or at Lydda airport, the language they heard, the idiom, the speech was Hebrew. In ten days children who previously had spoken French, German, Italian, Arabic, Hungarian, Rumanian, Polish, unable to understand one another, began to speak, haltingly to be sure but speaking nonetheless, the one tongue which made them all brothers and sisters.

In an accelerated effort to acquaint all with Hebrew, emergency classrooms were set up throughout the country. Special courses were offered for scientists, professionals and businessmen; and in a matter of months, 7,000 graduates of these special courses known as *ulpanim* learned enough basic Hebrew to practice law or medicine or to undertake office work. After winning its independence, the nation had to fight a desperate battle with time, it should be remembered. The immediate need was production, but how could an immigrant work at maximum efficiency without the indispensable tool of language? The *ulpanim* helped to reduce the wastage of human resources; the newspapers helped; each foreign language newspaper in Israel carries Hebrew lesson columns. A special paper for immigrants is written in voweled, uncomplicated Hebrew. A repertory theater group under government auspices travels the length and breadth of the land, presenting plays and musicals for the immigrants. The purpose of the drama is to introduce the newcomers visually and orally to the vigorous culture of their new country. The Voice of Israel, the nation's broadcasting network, schedules regular language lessons.

The culturalists who had fought for the spiritual rebirth of the state knew that the country had come of age when the *Knesset* created a free, compulsory, unified educational system. Under direction of the Ministry of Education, the "trend" system was abolished. Under that system, children had attended schools of one of four groups, each with its own cultural, political or religious orientation—General Zionist, Labor, Mizrachi, or Agudat Israel. Public schools in Israel today do not teach religion. Parents who want their children to have orthodox instruction may send them to state-aided religious schools. All schools must, however, give instruction in Hebrew. In 1955 Israel spent 13 per cent of its national budget for educational purposes.

In addition to free schools for agriculture and trade, the nation makes use of the army as a powerful instrument for universal education. The army takes in the raw recruit, the new immigrant, and puts him through a quick course in Hebrew and teaches him a trade of his own choice. Often it is in the army that an immigrant from some backward corner of the world—Yemen or North Africa, for example—learns for the first time the modern hygiene of the western world, the use of plumbing and sanitation such as he had never seen in his native land. The army, in teaching various trades, relates them both to military activity and to potential civilian use, so that the soldier, after military duty, is qualified to carry on and to earn his living. To acquire an understanding and love of the land, each recruit undergoes a period of agricultural training in border settlements, where under the program of *NAHAL* (Pioneering and Fighting Youth)—the badge combines both sword blade and scythe—he absorbs some national history and learns the technology of farming. Israel believes that this dual approach to military training makes better soldiers by making better-educated citizens.

Israel extends its educational facilities to all its citizens, including 180,000 Arabs. In 1955, 80 per cent of all Arab children of school age, about 28,000, attended

110 government Arab schools. In addition, mobile education units visit Arab farm communities, offering courses in reading and writing for Arab adults. Nothing resembling this comprehensive educational program exists for the masses in any Arab country.

Perhaps the most vivid evidence of the dynamism of the Jewish national movement is to be found in the establishment of the Hebrew University. At the end of the nineteenth century, there dawned the recognition of the need for a Jewish university where, for the first time, a true synthesis between general learning and specifically Jewish studies might be achieved. It seemed incredible that in modern times there should be no university founded, endowed and maintained by the People of the Book.

Such an institution for instruction and research, developing freely along independent lines, was to serve as a focus for the scientific and cultural aspirations of the Jews of Palestine and provide a center from which the Jewish contribution to world culture would radiate. Coming from a Jewish university—and from a Hebrew University in Jerusalem at that—the contribution would be recognized as that belonging particularly and classically to the Jewish people.

The idea gained ground with the spread of anti-Semitism, which made the position of Jewish students, scholars and scientists in many parts of the world increasingly difficult. At the beginning of the twentieth century, almost all the Jewish students in Russia and Rumania were barred by law from the universities of those countries. Elsewhere their admission to universities was limited. Similarly, in central Europe, normal university careers were being made difficult, if not impossible, for Jewish students solely because they were Jews.

Finally, after Field Marshal Lord Allenby had liberated the southern part of Palestine from the Turks in 1918, he was present to witness a stirring scene. In the distance, beyond Mount Scopus from which Titus had long ago directed the destruction of Jerusalem, British and Turkish guns boomed in duel. Field Marshal Allenby stood atop the mountain and watched the formal laying of the foundation stone of the Hebrew University by Dr. Weizmann, whose dream this had been for many years.

Seven years later, after the first three institutes (of chemistry, microbiology and Jewish studies) had been established, the university was formally opened in 1925. The dedication was celebrated by Lord Balfour, then seventy-six years of age, the man whose name meant so much in the establishment of Israel as an independent sovereign state, the man who signed his name to the Balfour Declaration. Balfour, despite his age, made the journey to Palestine solely for this purpose. Among the 7,000 persons who reverently attended this memorable ceremony were Chief Rabbi A. I. Kook of Palestine, the distinguished philosopher Ahad Ha'am, Chaim Nachman Bialik, the greatest of modern Hebrew poets, Lord Allenby, numerous statesmen, representing their governments, and an illustrious array of scholars and scientists from universities and academies in the four corners of the earth. Thus, in the shadow of the Holy City, while a war for its liberation still raged, the Jews, the People of the Book, consecrated a school of higher learning.

The university flourished and grew and stood over the old city like a fortress of the spirit. Then came the War of Independence. Professors and students were ambushed and murdered as they drove to their classrooms. Finally, the Armistice Agreement divided Mount Scopus from the state. Today the beautiful buildings on Mount Scopus stand, ghostly and still, under the hot sun of the Holy Land. But the university continues its work, although it has had to move its quarters several times. It functions in monasteries, lofts, abandoned warehouses, office buildings. In recent days magnificent new buildings have been built in the Israel sector of the city. The buildings of the new university will probably never equal the august and classical splendor of its old home on Mount Scopus. But the spirit within them, like the Jews' eternal quest for knowledge, throbs with the same passion.

The university, however, is not alone as an example of the renewed contributions of Israel to world learning. Great scientific and technical institutions like the Weizmann Institute and the Haifa Technion have been created with the assistance of Jewry outside Israel. These are now playing a notable part in atomic research and other aspects of physics. Medicine, which has always been a Jewish science, finds a home for healing and research in the magnificent new Hadassah hospital which is now rising outside Jerusalem.

Beyond the academic world, the resurgence of Israel has had a wide and beneficial impact. One of the most striking benefits of the renaissance of Hebrew culture has been to Jewish creative expression through the arts. The Israel Philharmonic Symphony Orchestra is recognized by all lovers of music as one of the world's great musical ensembles. A new Haifa Symphony is likewise winning national acclaim. Chamber music groups have sprung up all over the country in town and *kibbutz*. *Ein Gev*, a settlement on the shore of Lake Kinneret—the Biblical Sea of Galilee—is host to an annual music festival which attracts music lovers from many lands. This celebration takes place during the Passover week and in the spring of 1955 was especially devoted to the memory of the immortal teacher and philosopher, Maimonides, the 750th anniversary of whose death occurred during the year. The festival included the premiere of two plays: a musical, *Midor Ledor* ("From Generation to Generation"), and a historical play, *Hayad Hahazakah* ("The Strong Hand"), the title of Maimonides' code. A vigorous and talented Hebrew theater has also emerged in Israel and has branched out from the original *Habimah* players into various other groups such as *Ohel* and the Chamber Theater, which perform not only in the major cities but also in *kibbutzim*.

The revival of Jewish art in Israel is felt in all fields: in painting, the graphic arts and sculpture, as well as in many decorative skills. In the last named the Yemenite and Persian Jews, silversmiths, goldsmiths and artisans for centuries, have made their influence felt in jewelry, clothing, embroidery and all kinds of *objets d'art*.

Most important, many fine painters emigrated to Israel from Europe, bringing with them the techniques and skills of their native lands, of their native cultures— French, Hungarian, Rumanian. They now represent an older generation of what might be termed conservative painters. But out of the ferment and excitement of modern Israel, responsive to the extraordinary sharpness of light and shadow in that sunlit land, a younger generation of *sabra* painters—Israelis born in Israel who are more original and less derivative—has emerged, and more and more of their canvases are on display throughout Israel. Visitors to Safed, an artistic center in Galilee, see evidence of their talent at every turn.

# 6 THE MIRACLE OF ACHIEVEMENT

Talmudic sages admonished the Jewish people "not to rely on miracles," but to go forth and create them. Responsive to the original miracle of creation, a good Jew utters a prayer of thanks and, in a sense, of affirmation, in which he tells God that his own personal faith assures him that He will help him complete the undertaking.

The prayer book of Judaism does not encourage overindulgence in petitions. For centuries the Jews, an eminently realistic folk, have recognized that one cannot merely ask God for favors. Had their faith through the last two millennia rested upon fulfillment of such requests, Judaism as a faith would have long ago perished. The pious Jew acquiesced in the inscrutable way in which God works, and lived his life in the faith that God does bestow on man some means of human betterment. Build and prosper, the Jew believed, and thank God for the guidance, courage, and skill to achieve human goals: this is the core of Jewish messianism, which is rooted in a present, not a future world.

It was this optimism of spirit which breathed life into the Zionist movement. Without it, Jews in distant lands of exile would still be awaiting the Messiah while asking material salvation of the Creator. Zionism ennobled messianic belief by distinguishing between the basic physical needs of Jews and their spiritual needs. Zionism proclaimed that Jews would seek their own salvation, and at the same time await the Messiah. The Zionists stimulated Jewry to work and build instead of wait and sigh.

The dream and the challenge of Israel tested and proved the validity of this messianic faith. Reclaiming dead land, building power stations, factories, roads, industries—these tasks took on a spiritual as well as a material significance. No more fitting example exists than the challenge of the Huleh Valley project.

The Jordan River rises high in the Syrian mountains. Its sweet, cool waters tumble and fall some two hundred feet toward Lake Huleh in northern Galilee. Before the stream reaches the lake, it seeps into a large 7,000-acre marsh, breaks into hundreds of rivulets and turgid pools, twists and turns around the reeds and the rushes and is lost in the dismal swamps.

Above the swamps deadly mosquitoes drone. Around the reeds and the rushes live all varieties of wild life. Below the brackish waters lie vast accumulations of peat, the residue of thousands of years of strangled vegetation. The reeds thin out and the 3,000 acres of Lake Huleh come into sight. South of the lake the river fights its way tortuously through layers of black volcanic basalt and empties into the Sea of Galilee, six hundred feet below.

In a nation where land is so precious and water so pitifully scarce, the waste of the Huleh Valley is an intolerable loss. For thirty-five years people talked of draining the valley. A syndicate of Syrians had won, for £5,000, a concession from the Turkish Government to drain the swamps. They hoped to grow rich in the process, but could not raise the necessary capital for the drainage operation. Hence they were content to get rich more slowly by levying tolls for fishing and reed-cutting privileges. Twenty years later, in 1934, PICA bought the territory from these entrepreneurs for £P192,000. With the help of British engineers, PICA drew up ambitious plans to drain the swamp, but Arab disturbances and the outbreak of World War II halted operations. In the meantime, twenty small settlements in the area struggled for survival. Children with swollen bellies, men and women suffering from malarial palsy and fever proved that the Huleh mosquitoes were too much for the hardiest pioneers.

In 1951, the major assault on this pestilential area was launched. The plan called for a channel to be carved out of the inhibiting basalt. The stagnant waters from the lake and swamps would gush forth until all that was left would be a dried-out swamp, a smaller, deeper lake and a faster stream that would run clear and cool into the Sea of Galilee. The mosquitoes, deprived of their breeding grounds, would then vanish and with them the scourge of malaria. The unlimited supplies of peat would provide fuel and fertilizer for 15,000 acres of new farmland; and the water, instead of evaporating in the heat and dissipating itself into the swamps, would be returned for irrigating an additional 50,000 acres of land in the Negev.

The project was to be completed sometime in 1956. The mosquitoes still take their toll of the workers, and the workers also face the enmity of neighbors. A few hundred yards away across the border, Syrian troops keep watch as the engineers with their blueprints and tractors and bulldozers change the face of the land. A sudden pop and whine, and a worker falls dead over his wheel, the victim of a sniper's bullet. The Arabs, despite all entreaties, have also interfered with development south of Huleh, where a new channel is being dug for the river. Where a small triangle of Arab property interfered with the straight course of the river, the engineers had no alternative; they dug a new river bed around the property, contrary to every sane principle of engineering.

To the feudal Arabian landlord, the development of the Huleh stands as one more terrifying example of the Jewish spirit of enterprise. To drain a swamp in Israel, with a half dozen hostile neighbors peering across with hate at the operations, hardly leads to political tranquillity. The swamps grow cooler as they are drained, while the political climate grows ever hotter as the work progresses. Yet, despite harassment and bloodshed, the land will thrive. Bitter hatred, always part of the price of pioneering progress, cannot prevent that inevitable result. The Jews have built with love for the land. It is ironical that such love should have engendered such hatred.

The success of the Huleh project is an example of the venturesome spirit of Israel. This neglected land could hardly have been reclaimed through conventional profit motives. The costs would have been too high. And who could purchase land at exorbitant prices needed to repay the enormous investment required for private drainage contracts? At this stage in the development of Israel, the venture had to be a joint project of the labor of the people and the capital of the state. Private capital alone would not have undertaken the risk.

To continue the story of how the people of Israel are meeting the challenge of rebirth, one must visualize the chaos that confronted the young government on the day the British left the country. In 1948, the Israeli fleet consisted of a few antiquated vessels. The condition of the harbors was as inadequate as the merchant marine. The nation's single airport at Lydda had been abandoned by the British to the Arabs. All the international airlines, with no place to land, terminated their scheduled flights. Roads, blasted and gutted by war and neglect, were as much of a hazard as a help to communications. What little there was of a railway system was bombed and left to rust away, thus severing rail contact between the three main cities of the nation, Jerusalem, Tel Aviv and Haifa. When the British evacuated the Holy Land, they closed the post offices and the telegraph services. A few loyal volunteers kept the local telephone lines operating. British-controlled radio stations ceased functioning. Even such a humble service as "official time" ended with the departure of the Mandatory Power.

Yesterday the *Yishuv* had struggled against the hindrances imposed by a hostile occupying power. Today, that power had abdicated its authority, cut the community off from the rest of the world, and even from its component parts. Israel was left with its back to the sea to face seven invading nations.

War destroys, but it also creates. The war that 650,-000 Jews fought and won against 40,000,000 Arabs confirmed Israel's existence as a nation.

Self-doubts were erased in the course of the struggle. Clinging to the soil which they had learned through long hardships to reclaim from the desert and from the neglect of nearly 2,000 years, the Jews proved themselves to themselves. They could fight, they could endure and they could preserve, even enlarge, their tiny territory against the combined forces of the Arabs.

From that moment, no difficulties seemed insurmountable. There was a surge of self-confidence and a

new struggle born of unity. The tempo of life inside
Israel quickened, a steel-like energy infused all activity.
War, cruel though it is, furnished both stimulus and
binding force. Everybody, the women, the children,
those too old to fight, did their part; roads were built;
the telegraph system was patched up and made to function again. Temporarily without a navy, the country
had little need for harbor improvements. What little
remained of the new nation's communication system
took a dreadful battering from the guns of the Arab
Legion.

In the wake of its War of Liberation, which was not
of its own making, Israel was ready to devote itself to
the colossal tasks of upbuilding and the absorption of
the new immigrants. To understand the amplitude of
the achievement, one must understand the magnitude
of the challenge. That was seven years ago. Since then,
the battle-weary nation has taken in over 700,000 immigrants from sixty different countries. So vast and rapid
an increase would have been a heavy burden on the
economic system of any country, however prosperous.
Imagine the consequences if within a similar period the
United States had doubled its population.

Nevertheless, the immigrants were integrated into the
life of the country, into agriculture and into expanding
industry, into roadbuilding and reforestation. As fast as
one shipload of immigrants was absorbed another arrived. Today, the Jewish population of Israel numbers
about 1,600,000 or two and a half times as many Jews
as in 1948.

What complicated matters in Israel during the first years of its existence, was that by the elementary standards of any economic system, the nation was bankrupt. In 1948, it imported eight times as much as it exported. In succeeding years, its external trade position continued to deteriorate. For additional immigrants meant additional imports, and for some time the immigrants naturally produced little themselves.

During these years of one acute economic crisis after another, the trade gap was bridged mainly by American grants-in-aid, dollar loans from the Export-Import Bank, releases of frozen sterling balances, issuance of Israeli bonds, installments of restitution payments from Western Germany, thanks to the skillful and patient negotiations of Dr. Nahum Goldmann, chairman of the Jewish Agency and by gifts from world jewry. The last category paid for a third of all imports.

In spite of the efforts of Israeli cabinet members who spent much of their time abroad urging Jews to contribute more to the new state, it was impossible to maintain the gifts at the level of initial enthusiasm, or indeed increase them.

Moreover, high defense expenditures could not be curtailed as long as the Arab states persistently refused even to discuss peace treaties with Israel. On the contrary, in the face of mounting border attacks and violent threats from Israel's neighbors, caution and experience demanded an intensification of military preparedness.

What was to be done? In any other country, the logical answer would have been to suspend immigration until the nation was on a sound footing. But immigration is what Israel exists for; to deny it would be to abandon the Zionist cause and Israel's nationhood. Any Israeli government that even hinted at it would be thrown out of office in twenty-four hours.

That left only the alternative of reducing imports and raising exports. In order to enable Israeli exporters to compete abroad, the government was compelled to devaluate the Israeli pound, which formerly rated internationally at the same level as sterling. Simultaneously, the Israeli industrial worker had to produce more. The workers in town and country had worked strenuously to build the new state. Yet, their productive capacity was 30 per cent below that of western Europe because of lack of modern equipment and methods which made productivity low in industry.

The land of "milk and honey" was also known in Biblical days as the land "whose stones are iron and out of whose hills thou mayest dig brass." The new nation has a long road to travel. Three quarters of a billion dollars of goods which Western Germany has agreed in penance to contribute will help to pay the way, distasteful as it is for many Israelis to accept German reparation. The financial "wizards" in the government stabilized currency and controlled exports. They passed laws enforcing savings and imposing a necessary period of austerity. All these measures will help balance the people's living needs at the level which they can afford through production.

Yet, in spite of all remedial measures, coupled with a ruthless austerity program, Israel is still unable to survive without outside aid, and still more help is needed to assure survival.

For the West, Israel is both politically and economically a good risk. It is the only democratic and internally stable nation in the Middle East. It believes in the same political principles as Americans do. Its people is equal in character and caliber to that of any western country. Its army is already the most powerful military force in the Middle East and grows stronger with each year of Israel's economic progress.

*"Yih'yeh beseder"* (it will be all right) is the immediate answer to all who wonder whether the prodigious feats needed can be accomplished. In this sense, Israel is the abiding token of the triumphant survival of the Jewish people.

By the end of the war, a network of communications stretched across the country. Desert was linked to sea coast, city to mountain, plain to harbor. The ports were dredged. Haifa, the greatest port in the Eastern Mediterranean, now has a gigantic floating crane, the largest in the Middle East. The Israeli merchant marine operates thirty-five ships under its own flag manned by some 1,500 Israeli-trained men. Visitors fly in and out of the country by El Al, an Israeli-owned airline. Aircraft land and take off at four airdromes, which are in process of expansion. A railroad from the Negev will handle the heavy mineral freight from the desert to the cities and the cities of Israel are now linked by rail.

In the southern Negev, evidences of King Solomon's copper mines and smelting foundries have been excavated. During the nervous days immediately before independence, Britain and the United States tried to induce the leaders of the Yishuv to give up the Negev. Those tough-minded men remembered what had been, stood firm and refused. They recalled the prosperity of Solomon's kingdom and its successful exploitation of the Negev mines. The nation needed this promising frontier, a territory rich in minerals, to provide raw materials for industry.

The creation and development of a metal industry requires an intricate organization of subsidiary enterprises. Manufacturing cannot precede the exploitation of the mineral deposits through a mining industry. A chemical industry is dependent upon raw material and power. If industry is located in the desert it needs a steady water supply. A system of roads and shipping and internal communications must function efficiently. In such a small country, when one link breaks, the whole national enterprise may collapse. After much toil and ingenuity, the Negev is now fulfilling each day the high hopes held out for it.

The Israel Mining Corporation, established by the government in 1951, has discovered in the Negev deposits of manganese, copper, phosphates, glass sand, ball clay, mica, feldspar, iron, gypsum, clay. So rapidly had the phosphate industry grown by 1954, that imports of the mineral ceased. Very soon a giant chemical plant will be built in the Negev to produce sulphuric acid, calcined phosphates, soda ash, phosphoric acid, phosphatic salts and concentrated fertilizers, all from Negev and Dead Sea resources. Before independence, the Dead Sea was the nation's only mining area. The northern plant was seized by Jordan and is out of action, but that at Sodom produced over 18,000 tons in 1954.

The varied clays found in the Negev should provide the basis for a prosperous ceramics industry. Its silicon sands will soon make Israel a glass-exporting nation. So far no oil deposits have been discovered in Israel, but geological surveys have proved encouraging, and nine companies are drilling for oil.

The stability of the government, its respect for international treaties as well as an intelligent labor force, have encouraged large-scale foreign investment. According to a survey published by the U. S. Department of Commerce, a total of $54 million of private American investment capital went to Israel during the five-year period, 1949-1953. These investments include mainly U. S. equity in foreign corporations, foreign branches of American corporations, sole proprietorships, partnerships and real property. For example, Kaiser-Frazier is assembling automobiles in Haifa, while the General Tire and Rubber Company (Israel) Ltd. and the Alliance Tire and Rubber Company Ltd. produce tires in Petah Tikvah.

Locally owned companies supply all of the electrical power the country needs in spite of the considerably increased consumption which rose from 464 million KWH in 1950 to 895 m. KWH in 1954. Almost all electrical appliances are home-produced. Frames for the largest pipes in the world, forged to carry water through the desert, roll out of a steel mill in Acre in the north. Supplies for the building industry are made entirely in Israel—cement, lime, plaster, bricks, plywood, paints, varnishes, marble, granite, basalt, limestone and safety glass.

Israel's economic planners aim in two parallel directions. They hope that within a few years Israel will be wholly able to feed itself even with a population of 2,000,000 expected by 1960. To this end, the area under cultivation has been expanded from 413,000 acres in 1948 to almost 1,000,000 in 1954, and the land under irrigation has increased threefold since 1948 and is now above 200,000 acres. Israel's agricultural production today compares favorably already with any country in the world. The striking progress made in Israel's agriculture was described by Levi Eshkol, Israel Minister of Finance, at the beginning of 1955. "We are producing all the vegetables, all the fruit, and all the dairy products and poultry we need," Mr. Eshkol said. Within the last six years, he added, agricultural output had more than doubled, and exports had risen considerably.

During the last season, Israel exported 8,200,000 cases of citrus fruits, yielding over $35 million in foreign exchange. Peanut plantations, almost unknown to Israel's farmers a few years ago, will produce a crop of 15,000 tons in 1955, over half of which will be sold in Europe. Cotton planting is no longer an experiment

but a genuine success. British experts have estimated
that the quality of Israeli cotton is equal to the best in
the world.

Highly significant was Mr. Eshkol's statement with
regard to the vocational restratification of the immigrants. "Agriculture is not simply a question of crops
and land. It is also a question of people. New crops have
been introduced but we have had even more spectacular
results in introducing new people to the land. Since
1948, close to 30,000 families have settled on the land
and are becoming rooted."

The maximum effort for the intensification of the
agricultural production—a factor of paramount importance for Israel's economy—is matched only by the re-
lentless drive to reduce the trade deficit. In 1951, Israel
was importing at the rate of $390 million a year. In
1954, imports were more than $100 million below this
figure, despite the fact that the population simultaneously increased by 200,000 persons. On the other hand,
exports increased nearly 50 per cent to $85 million, thus
reducing the trade gap by 9 per cent, to $203 million.
These figures reflect Israel's economic growth, but the
fact remains that despite this improvement, Israel still
imports three times as much as she exports.

To surmount roadblocks in its path toward the goal
of a balanced, self-supporting economy, Israel had to
develop those types of industries for which technologi-
cal skill is rare in its geographical area. Foremost among
these manufacturing enterprises are spindle mills for
the production of fine cotton yarns, factories for air

conditioning, refrigeration and radio units, precision
instruments, fine glass and ceramics articles, for dia-
mond cutting and polishing, for metallurgical products
and similar commodities for a worldwide market.

The crucial need for an expanded export market was
duly recognized by the Histadrut—the Israel Federation
of Labor—certainly the most unusual labor organization in the world. Formed during the days of the Mandate by socialist-labor idealists, Histadrut proposed to
guarantee the rights of the laboring classes and also to
influence the nation's business so that the Israeli worker
would eventually live a comfortable, secure life in a
cooperative commonwealth. Accordingly, Histadrut in-
vested its funds in a *Chevrat Ovdim*, a workers' company, which built industrial enterprises, managed them,
and employed Histadrut workers. None of the profits
were to go into private hands; instead they were to be
reinvested in new industry.

Histadrut expanded into cooperatives on the land.
Some cooperatives are in partnership with Histadrut,
which owns 51 per cent of the shares, the rest belonging to the resident members. Others are wholly owned
by Histadrut. The profits from such ventures are turned
back to cooperative funds for reinvestment. Likewise,
Histadrut owns outright some industrial companies
and is also in partnership with private venture capital in
others.

For most labor union members in other countries the
activities of Histadrut would seem like strange ventures
for a labor union. And in fact they are. Where else in

the world does a trade union train foreign workers for jobs in its country, help them to immigrate, and put them to work even on competition with its own members in its own factories? It may seem strange when compared with labor unions in established countries, where unions seek only a fair share of profit from established industries. And this is the crux of the matter: Histadrut did not grow in an established industrial society. In the early development of the country's economy, Histradut found itself with too few industries, too few investors to finance them, no government to encourage them and, sometimes, without skilled labor to operate them if they did develop. To give workers employment Histadrut had to create industry. To guarantee that the industry would flourish, Histadrut had to train and import a labor force. To guarantee that a fair balance existed between both, Histadrut had to serve the requirements of both management and labor.

Histadrut leaders assumed decisive roles in the campaign for independence. They played a leading role in the organization of the *Haganah*. In the days of travail, they planned and executed daring moves by which thousands of "illegals" were spirited into the country. Today, Histadrut provides a great network of health centers and cultural and educational institutions.

The efficient and disciplined structure of Histadrut served the cause of national renaissance magnificently. But now that Israel is an established state, say critics of Histadrut, the government should assume all the manifold functions of Histadrut and take over its health centers, trade schools, clinics, dispensaries and health insurance plans. Many of the new immigrants do not feel altogether comfortable as members of a union which also owns the factory. Against whom does one strike if one is dissatisfied? And where is the instrument for the strike? The union officials are also the managers of the company. The problem as yet has not been solved, but in the next decade or so a clear and fair evaluation of the role of Histadrut in Israeli life will certainly evolve.

At the moment its role is a vital one. Histadrut employs 40,000 workers in its industries. A half million people are members. To disband or nationalize its industrial enterprise, as some suggest, would create immediate complications. The government is deeply involved in its own endeavors. And the creative zeal of the Histadrut leaders, the same labor-industrial pioneers who built when there was nothing, is a dynamic force in the nation's progress. Israel cannot afford to lose such dynamism and ignore such achievement.

What will guarantee economic success for Israel is not good luck or wit, but will. The people who love the land are being enriched by its redemption. They will endure hard work and meager returns, heavy taxation and privations so that someday their children may see a better day.

# 7 LIVING UNDER LAW

Israel's Declaration of Independence proclaimed to all mankind the fundamental principles of the new state. This document opened the doors of the state to the free immigration of Jews from all over the world. In its dedication to the ideal of law in its highest ethical sense, in its recognition of the dignity of the individual, in its concept of the emancipation of women, a revolutionary development in the Middle East, in its recognition of human freedom, it was a remarkable document to be issued in a backward area of the world which is still one of the last strongholds of feudalism.

It pledged a government, based on the principles of liberty, justice and peace, for the benefit of every citizen, without distinction as to race, color or sex. It vowed to uphold the full social and political equality of all its citizens. It guaranteed freedom of religion, conscience, education and culture; pledged itself to protect the holy places of all religions; and committed itself to uphold the principles of the United Nations Charter.

The founders of modern Israel knew full well that these principles harmonized naturally with the Zionist ideal of Jewish rebirth. They were part and parcel of the great ethical concepts of Judaism. Rabbi Abba Hillel Silver describes Judaism as being "concerned with the unchanging needs of man and society, the needs which take on new forms in new settings but which remain fundamentally the same. . . . From Abraham and Moses there stretches an unbroken chain of spiritual continuity. . . . Each generation faced the same problem: how to achieve freedom under the sovereignty of God, justice under the mandate of His law and dignity in kinship with Him. . . ."

To a believing Jew, this unbroken continuity of concern with justice and freedom calls on each new generation to consider the demands of social and personal ethics as religious obligations. Man must strive for ethical perfection just as he must strive to serve God. If man is imperfect and in need of guidance, the laws of God stand to light the way, for His law embodies, to quote Rabbi Silver again, "changeless principles in mutable forms . . . the fixed points of reference for each generation."

Since Judaism concerns itself with the vital principles

of human conduct and society, the founders of Israel were true to their deepest convictions in their commitment to a government based upon law and the ideal of law in its highest democratic connotation.

The State, it must be remembered, was invaded by its neighbors at the very moment of its establishment. If, under these circumstances, the founders of Israel had decided to rule by military decree, concentrating all power in their own hands, many would have accepted this as an inevitable necessity. But this temptation was pushed aside: almost immediately the Provisional Government established a Supreme Court, laid the foundations of an independent judiciary, and prepared for a first general election which was held as soon as a census could be taken. This election took place on January 25, 1949, only eight months after establishment of the state, and while Israel was still under assault by its enemies.

The results were significant; for of a population of 782,000 people, 87 per cent of those eligible to vote cast their ballots and elected, by proportional representation which gave voice to all groups, a *Knesset*—or parliament—of 120 members. Every man and woman, over the age of eighteen, was eligible to vote. The moderate socialist Mapai, the largest labor party of the nation and the architect of Histadrut, the chief trade union, polled more than a third of the vote. The vote for the leftist Mapam, 14 per cent, reflected early friendship felt toward Russia because she had voted for Israel's statehood in the United Nations. This party later lost ground. The religious bloc won 13 per cent and Herut, representing the extreme nationalist groups, 11 per cent. The General Zionists, advocating free private enterprise and a unified national education, polled only 5 per cent. (In 1951 this party received 16 per cent of the votes.) A dozen smaller parties divided the rest of the vote.

The members of the single-chamber *Knesset* were elected for terms of four years. They were to confirm in office a cabinet of thirteen, headed by a prime minister, appointed by the president. The cabinet's tenure of office depended on the confidence of the *Knesset*.

David Ben-Gurion, the first prime minister, rejected a coalition with the extreme leftists. He organized a cabinet consisting of his Mapai party with seven seats, the religious bloc with three, the Progressives with one, and the Sephardic Jews with one.

It was an eventful year. The United Nations admitted Israel to membership, and this old-new nation became once more a member of the comity of nations. The *Knesset* directed a constitutional committee to draft articles which, as accepted by the *Knesset*, were to become the constitution of Israel. The government, acting upon a resolution of the *Knesset*, proclaimed that Jerusalem would be the capital of the nation, as it had been in ancient days. A conscription law, requiring national service from men and unmarried women between the ages of eighteen and twenty-six was passed. After a period of basic military training, each recruit was required to serve a year in agriculture. As the population reached the million mark, the *Knesset* voted to provide free and compulsory education for all the nation's children.

The issue of free and compulsory education focused national attention on the tensions between the religious and lay parties. The former sought to include in the public school curriculum instruction in the Jewish religion (and in the Arab schools, Christianity and Islam), while the latter opposed enforced religious education in the public schools. The first Ben Gurion government fell on this issue for it seemed to both sides that it was not merely the future of the public school system but the entire social and cultural configuration of the state that was at stake.

The ensuing campaign led to a discussion of basic issues of national policy—of the kind of state Israel should be. A fundamental question was the extent of rabbinical authority, in view of the profound attachment of the nation to Jewish tradition, and the fear of some that a theocracy would ultimately develop. Tacitly the government confirmed the rabbinate's authority, which it had enjoyed under the Mandate, over marriage, divorce, and standards of dietary laws.

In fact, however, the question of a so-called theocratic state is more academic than real, for Judaism has no church or clerical hierarchy; there is no central governing authority in Judaism; there is no chain of command.

The question of religion and the state is peculiarly complicated in Israel, as Ben Gurion, the lay leader, has pointed out:

"The problem of religion in Israel is not similar to that of Church and State in Christian countries. The Jewish faith differs fundamentally from Christianity. It does not rest satisfied with abstract religious principles; it is based on *mitzvoth*, on specific commandments as to what shall be done and what shall not be done, which comprehend the life of man from the moment of birth and—even earlier—until death and burial, leaving no neutral area outside the field of religion. At the same time the Jewish religion is national in character; it has absorbed all the historic elements in the life of the Jewish people from the time it came into being until this day. And it is not easy to separate the national from the religious aspect. . . . The fusion of the religious and national elements is nothing new in our history; it is as old as Israel itself. . . . America has adopted the convenient solution of separating Church from State, not for anti-religious reasons, but on the contrary, because of a deep attachment to religion and the desire to secure full religious freedom for each and every citizen. But this would not solve the problem if it were applied to Israel.

"A talent for compromise," the first prime minister went on, "is a vital condition for the existence of any community. . . . It is clear that in our times it is not absolutely necessary to make final decisions on matters of opinion and faith on which we shall continue to differ for a long time to come. . . . An uncompromising struggle regarding the status of religion in the state, or attempts at coercion in matters of religion, are liable to serve as explosive material in the national life and, in the best of cases, must delay the process of inner fusion which is the vital need and preliminary condition for the survival of Israel."

The spirit of compromise, however, would not satisfy extremists on both sides. For groups such as *Hashomer Hatzair* (The Young Watchmen), secular socialism is the only true religion and any compromise with the demands of past or present is a betrayal of the future. On the other hand, the tiny and fanatical *N'turei Karta* (Guardians of the City), in Jerusalem's *Mea Shearim* quarter, regard compromise as blasphemy. Indeed, isolated in time, the *N'turei* group refuses to recognize the authority of the Israel government, holding that only the Messiah can bring about a Jewish state. The *N'turei Karta* is cited here not as a representative group, but as an example of an extreme point of view.

The 1951 election was a victory for Ben-Gurion and the tacit compromise he advocated became assured national policy. "In order to prevent a religious war," he had said, his government had to prevent "either a war for religion or a war against religion."

The prime minister invited Mapam and the General Zionists into his cabinet, but the two parties' diametrically opposite demands indicated that an effective government would have been impossible. Again Ben-Gurion turned to the religious parties. The new, unstable coalition cabinet splintered over the issue of national service for women. Despite a compromise on that issue, Ben Gurion could not muster a majority in the *Knesset,* and in December, 1952, he brought the General Zionists into the cabinet. The following summer, the *Knesset* passed the State Education Law which did away with the four-party trend schools and provided for a unified educational system. Those who wished to send their children to private schools might do so, providing that they met the national educational standard. Religious schools would likewise receive state support.

That same year the *Knesset* enacted the Judges' Law, separating the judiciary from the executive; the law provided that the president with the advice of a special committee would appoint judges from those who fulfilled prescribed requirements. In November, the *Knesset* passed the National Insurance Law, Israel's first comprehensive health, welfare and social security legislation. Writs of habeas corpus and mandamus in force during the British occupation were reconfirmed. Other laws were enacted abolishing the death penalty and corporal punishment, except in the case of Nazi war criminals. A Women's Equal Rights Law, outlawing polygamy and child marriages, was passed to secure the rights of women among oriental Jews. By the beginning of 1954, when David Ben Gurion resigned as prime minister because of "extreme weariness," it had become clear that the legislative machinery of the country was firmly established. Few believed that a patriot as devoted as Ben Gurion would give up responsibilities in a period of instability; and indeed, in 1955, he returned, after months spent as a pioneer in a Negev settlement, to become Minister of Defense.

Israel's government today is, like that of Great Britain, without a written constitution. The Declaration of Independence serves as a kind of preamble—similar to that of the United States—to the constitution that would evolve. Those laws in force under the Mandate were to remain the laws of the land unless they conflicted with the Law and Administrative Ordinance, or were later repealed by the *Knesset*. What was the basis of the law under the Mandatory? The British governed the country under a thoroughly consistent legal system during most of the thirty years of their administration in Palestine. Not even the customary indifference of colonial armies could destroy British pride in the sanctity of the law and its traditions. Above all, the British are, and respect, law-abiding people, and except for the few years preceding independence, their government was a government of strict and efficient justice.

Much of the basic law during the Mandate was derived from English Common Law. However, since the Mandate dealt with three religious groups, the law had to take into account the customs and habits of Moslems as well as Christians and Jews. Before the Mandate, Palestinians had lived under Moslem law administered by Turkish authority. Some of those laws are still in force; others, not in accord with needs of a modern country, have been repealed. For example, Moslem law is greatly concerned with donkeys, camels, horses and cows, but there is little legislation relating to locomotives, airplanes, cars and steamships. Specific judgments, of which the following is an example, give guidance as to how Moslem law judges litigations in which animals are involved:

A donkey gambols about and splashes mud on a passerby. He also kicks with his heels and causes serious injury. For this, the animal's owner is not to be considered legally responsible. But if the owner is riding the animal and it inflicted injury with the front legs and the head, the rider is responsible. The owner is not responsible for damage done by the animal's rear parts.

Here is another case cited by the Honorable Shneour Zalman Cheshin, deputy president of Israel's Supreme Court:

The owner of a pearl worth fifty piastres drops it and it is swallowed by a hen worth five piastres; the owner of the pearl may take the hen upon the payment of five piastres.

This case provides legal guidance regarding neighborly relations:

If a person climbs up the fruit trees in his garden, and thereby overlooks the women's quarters of his neighbor, such a person must give information every time he intends to climb such trees in order that the women may cover themselves. Should he fail to give such information the court may forthwith prohibit him from climbing such trees. . . .

This reflects Moslem tradition requiring women to cover their faces. Under Turkish law, violation of this edict incurs punishment.

Laws of evidence, according to Turkish law, reflected the attitude of the Orient toward women generally: "In civil cases evidence is only valid when given by two males or by one male and two females." This is an example of a statute rendered obsolete by Israel's Women's Equal Rights Law of 1951.

Wherever there were gaps in the Turkish law, the British filled in with English Common Law. This is accepted in Israel and used as the base of the legal structure. From a juridical standpoint, the British and the Israelis are in accord.

Four significant cases came before the Israel Supreme Court as cited by Justice Cheshin in a paper presented to the Bar Association of the City of New York, December, 1954. The first involved the Minister of the Interior, who has the right to suspend a publication if it prints material tending to undermine the security of the state or to render insecure the peace of its citizens. He must, however, specify the term of the suspension.

Not long ago the minister suspended two papers, one Arabic, the other Hebrew, for some weeks for criticizing the foreign policy of the country. The minister held that Israel was practically in a state of siege and could ill afford such disruptive influence. The Israel court, relying upon precedent established by Justices Brandeis and Holmes of the United States Supreme Court, cited Brandeis' opinion in his famous *Whitney vs. the People*

*of the State of California* in rendering its decision:
"Those who won our independence believe that . . .
freedom to think as you will and to speak as you think
are means indispensable to the discovery and spread
of political truth; that without free speech and assembly,
discussion would be futile. . . . Only an emergency
can justify repression of free expression. Such must be
the rule if authority is to be reconciled to freedom."

The persuasiveness of this argument and its applica-
bility to the spirit of Israel moved the court to direct the
minister to cancel his order of suspension. The court
agreed that the writings might have been subversive,
and conceded that the country was in a state of war.
But it concluded that these facts could not justify the
destruction of the basic principle of freedom of the
press.

Another case concerned an Israeli Arab who was held
in military prison by an army commander. Access to his
family, his attorney or his friends was not permitted.
The family appealed to the Supreme Court. The court
stated that the special regulations which permitted the
commander, in times of emergency, to apprehend an
individual suspected of subversive actions, also obli-
gated him to make the conditions of that arrest known
to the attorney and family of the detained.

There was also the plaintive situation of the elderly
married Arab who fell in love with a young lady and
wished to marry her, arguing that his religion permitted
him more than one wife. The *Kadi*, religious judge of the
Moslems, refused on the grounds that this would violate

the civil law. The would-be bridegroom retorted that this was a violation of his own religious rights, and protested too that he had paid a high price to the father of the girl. Again the court turned to American case history, involving Mormon multiple marriage. The Supreme Court of Israel decided that the Moslem religion permitted but did not enjoin him to marry more than one wife. Thus, in denying him the right to set aside the Women's Equal Rights Law, the court was in no way violating his religious rights.

Another decisive case involved a school teacher who was dismissed from his post by the Director of Education by order of the Minister of Defense because the teacher had allegedly held revolutionary ideas and had also, before statehood, been a leader in a revolutionary movement. In effect, the court told the minister to mind his own business, the matter was properly the concern of the Director of Education. To dismiss a man on order of the Minister of Defense indicated that the man's case was not properly evaluated by the Director of Education under whose responsibility the accused worked. The court found that the teacher's civil rights had been impaired and ordered that he be permitted to return to his post.

These four cases, of course, disclose only some aspects of the law in Israel. But far beyond such cases is the everyday significance of the Law by which Israel and its people live today: a fusion of the ideals of the prophets of ancient Israel with the most advanced ideas of the twentieth century; the emphasis upon human rights, social justice, and peace, the three major pillars of Judaism through the ages; the recognition that democracy demands that social and economic problems be the concern of both government and people; the dedication to the moral and political tradition of an ancient people which find its ideal in a living, workable, democratic Law. Pierre Van Paassen once described the Jewish people as one "which has its life and being in two concepts—unity in the law of this world and hope in the final triumph of justice." It is an appraisal which the visitor to modern Israel finds apt.

# 8 "... AND THERE IS NO PEACE"

It is ironical that Israel should have been besieged by war from the day of its birth. The prophetic ideal of peace is the heart and soul of Zionism. Jews have always believed that God's blessings would come to those who would "beat their swords into plow-shares and their spears into pruning hooks; nations shall not raise up sword against nation, neither shall they learn war any more." The Psalmist envisioned the day of fulfillment when "mercy and truth are met together, righteousness and peace shall have kissed each other. Truth shall spring out of the earth and righteousness shall look down from heaven."

Yet, Israel has known anything but peace. The new nation is surrounded by neighbors who vow not peace but the sword. Shortly after his coronation, on November 12, 1953, the new King Saud of Saudi Arabia declared, "Israel, to the Arab world, is like a cancer to the human body, and the only way to remedy it is to uproot it just like a cancer. Israel is a serious wound in the Arab world body and we cannot endure the pain of this wound forever. . . . We Arabs total about 50,000,000. Why don't we sacrifice 10,000,000 of our number and live in pride and self-respect?"

What causes the ruler of a state to urge that 10,000,-000 of his people should be sacrificed in the cause of pride and self-respect? Whence emanates the violent bitterness which inspired an Arab diplomat in London to declare, "The Arabs are willing to wait ten, fifteen, twenty or twenty-five years for their revenge. . . . The hatred of the Arabs will last forever." What led the former Syrian representative at the Security Council of the United Nations to boast, "40,000,000 Arabs have the power to throw 1,000,000 Jews into the sea. . . . This is the only chance to heal the wound inflicted on our hearts by the disaster of Palestine."

The answer is not simple. There is surely a combination of genuine hatred and personal shame in these bitter threats. But these intemperate words find sympathetic audience among the Arab masses, and the Arab potentates consider that they have much to gain by fomenting ever greater enmity against Israel. An external enemy has always proven vital to the security of dictators. So long as the *fellahin* hate Israel, domestic oppression will not occupy their minds.

During the Arab-Israel war, the military potential of such hatred was tested and found wanting. The morale of any people cannot depend only on negative ill will; the outnumbered Israelis, fighting for a cause, could hold any field courageously against Arabs who had no cause but to destroy, no gain in victory, no loss in defeat. Yet the Arab potentates continue to stand by the ensign of hatred rampant on a field of corruption.

Relations with the Arabs have not always been so tense and bitter. During the first thirty years of Jewish settlement in Palestine, the two peoples lived relatively peacefully together. From time to time, Bedouin would attack a frontier settlement in order to murder and plunder. But they did not limit themselves to Jews; had the pickings been equally as good there they would just as readily have assaulted an Arab settlement.

Nothing that suggested a "Holy War" was in evidence. The Arabs far outnumbered the Jews of the *Yishuv*. Like most Middle Eastern peoples, Palestine's Arabs were absorbed with the necessity of scratching a living from the soil and rearing children in the face of debilitating disease. The Jews brought new agricultural methods and shared their knowledge with the *fellahin*; Arab harvests yielded increasing produce. Jewish doctors treated Arabs who suffered from trachoma; they administered medicines to keep baby and mother alive after childbirth. The Palestinian Arab became relatively prosperous economically, compared to his brother in Jordan, Syria and Egypt. He worshiped peacefully in his mosque; and he spoke his own language.

In the ten years before Israel's independence, the country suffered from repeated clashes between Arabs and Jews. These conflicts left a legacy of bitterness. This appeared especially tragic when it was proven that the Mufti's extremists had fomented most of the violence. Frequently the Arab attackers came from outside Palestine; they slipped across the border in the dead of night, poisoned wells, murdered, and then slipped away. Other terrorists took orders from leaders of a small cabal within the country. The majority of the Palestine Arab population swallowed the propaganda and remained at peace.

Because of this, Israel's leaders hoped that after Independence, they could live peacefully with Palestinian Arabs, freed from violence instigated from abroad. They offered guarantees of civil rights and security for Arabs in Israel, as proof of a sincere desire to live in peace on an equal basis with the country's Arab population.

The Declaration of Independence contained the following plea:

"WE APPEAL—in the very midst of the onslaught launched against us now for months—to the Arab inhabitants of the State of Israel to preserve peace and participate in the rebuilding of the state on the basis of full and equal citizenship and due representation in all its provisional and permanent institutions.

"WE EXTEND our hand to all neighboring States and their peoples in an offer of peace and good neighborliness, and appeal to them to establish bonds of cooperation and mutual help with the sovereign Jewish people settled in their own land. The State of Israel is prepared to do its share in a common effort for the advancement of the entire Middle East."

This entreaty failed. Before actual hostilities began, wealthy Arabs were already leaving the country to spend the summer in Lebanon, telling those who stayed that, within a few months, the Arab armies would drive the Jews into the sea. When this objective was achieved, they could return. The Arab League broadcast instructions to the Arab population in Israel, warning them to leave the country immediately or face punishment as traitors when victory was complete. As the armies and air forces of six nations began the assault, panic gripped Israel's Arab population. The war had been described to them as a war of extermination.

Utterly without confidence in their own leaders (most of whom had fled) and hysterically afraid of what the Israelis might do to them should they win in that war of extermination, the Israeli Arabs started running.

Wherever the Israeli armies advanced rapidly, as in Galilee, the Arab population preferred to stay. In the border region and in the areas of protracted fighting, the invaders told them to escape. By the end of the war more than 600,000 refugees were encamped on the borders of Israel, living in the most abject kind of squalor. Their reluctant host countries would have allowed them to perish had the United Nations not intervened with food and supplies.

Immediately before statehood and during and after the war, the Israeli government had opened the gates to all Jews who wished to settle in the country. Almost as many immigrants entered the country during this period as there were Arabs who had evacuated it. Despite the swollen population, an overstrained economy, and national weariness after the war, the Israel government offered to take back 100,000 of the refugees, and to accept the full burden of reintegrating them into Israeli society, if the Arab nations would take care of the rest and discuss a permanent peace.

The utter refusal of the Arabs to consider this generous offer revealed their purpose. The fact that Arab governments had forced the exile of the entire Jewish communities of Yemen, Iraq and Syria, and had expropriated their possessions did not mitigate the Arab demands. They demanded the impossible: All refugees were to be returned and the full cost for their rehabilitation was to be borne by Israel. They knew that this exorbitant demand would be rejected. The refugees would then become a pawn in the Arab game of power politics. By keeping them at the level of bare subsistence, as a sick, homeless, embittered mass, the Arab leaders hoped to fix the blame for their plight on the new state. And in some measure, they have enjoyed greater success with this than in their military effort, for the conscience of the world cannot help but be moved by the situation of hundreds of thousands of ragged, homeless people.

Abba Eban, Israel's Ambassador to the United Nations, has stated the position of his government on the refugee question. He has asked that open, free negotiations be initiated to liquidate all outstanding grievances between Arab states and Israel. Israel was willing to release the blocked bank accounts of Arab refugees (amounting to approximately $10 million). It was also willing to cooperate in resettling a reasonable number of refugees and particularly to reunite family groups. It expressed full willingness to pay adequate compensation to the Arabs for the land they had left. One would be hard put to find a historical parallel in history for a victorious nation's indemnifying its defeated enemy voluntarily. The Jewish refugees who left Iraq, Yemen and Syria not only were forced to surrender all their property but, in some cases, were also forced to pay a per capita tax for the privilege of leaving. For most of the impoverished emigrants, Jewish relief agencies had to pay this ransom.

The primary condition which the Israeli government demanded in exchange for this offer was that the Arab governments would negotiate peace in a spirit of good will. To demonstrate this spirit Israel demanded that the blockade against Israel imposed by the Arab League be raised. The blockade had closed the Suez Canal to Israeli shipping, and had forbidden free trade between the Arab states and Israel. It had closed the borders of any Arab state to any individual who held an Israel visa. The effect of the blockade was to deny the advantages of cultural, political or economic contact to Israel and to its neighbors alike.

The same bitterness that inspired the blockade has precipitated or encouraged hundreds of border clashes since the end of the war, which have caused thousands of deaths and injuries and enormous losses in property. Ill will has prevented all the nations of the area from utilizing for the benefit of all natural resources such as rivers and watersheds. The loss in irrigation and electrical energy, so desperately needed by the entire region, is incalculable. In a spirit of forgiveness, said Eban, no problem between Israel and the Arab countries could go unsolved, and the entire Middle East would gain.

To every plea, the Arab nations remained unmoved. Before they would consent even to consider an agenda for discussion, they demanded that every refugee Arab be resettled in his former home, and that all responsibility for reintegration be charged to Israel. By demanding the impossible, the Arab states served notice that they wished not peace but the continuation of war.

Despite this intransigence, Israel has behaved with good faith toward its own Arabs. By 1955, the Arab population of Israel had increased to 180,000 from 100,000 at the end of the war. The Arab economic and political situation has continued to improve. In the second *Knesset* there were eight Arab members; the Israel government encourages the Arab womenfolk to vote by providing separate voting booths and separate voting time for them, in deference to the Arab custom of separating the sexes in public places. Social agencies are helping to integrate the Arab population, and Histadrut has found them jobs, lent them funds for farm equipment and generally sought to ease their economic plight.

Laws relating to compulsory education and health standards benefit Arabs as well as Jews. Literacy is on the ascendancy and disease on the decline. In their schools Israeli Arabs speak and learn in their own language; even in the *Knesset* they have the same right. They are first-class citizens of Israel enjoying all civil rights. There are some Arabs who resent the laws which prevent them from taking more than one wife or from selling a child into marriage before her maturity. But even these restrictions have not greatly impeded the pursuit of happiness for most Israeli Arabs.

The attitude of Christian Arabs toward Israel was recently expressed by Monsignor George Hakim of Nazareth. "We feel as free and happy," he said, "as if we were living in a purely Christian country."

The Israeli government still admits certain refugees when family conditions warrant and when facilities for absorption permit. Israel has already paid out to refugees (in 1955) more than $2.5 million of blocked bank accounts and expects to continue payments until the balance of the $10 million is fully returned, despite the Arab refusal to consider peace proposals of which this was an essential part. The government still stands ready to negotiate compensation for abandoned Arab lands.

What have the Arab states actually done for their refugees? In every Arab state, except one, where refugees are situated, the governments regard them as aliens. They have not been granted citizenship, economic, or social rights. Refugees must look to the United Nations for support. They are discouraged by their fellow Arabs in host countries from engaging in industry, purchasing land or otherwise building a new life for themselves.

There are surely adequate facilities for integrating the refugees. The Arab nations possess 2,500,000 square miles of territory, much of it unsettled land of potential fertility. Saudi Arabia alone occupies more than 900,000 square miles of land. Its king rides in air-conditioned limousines over his desert roads, builds himself railroads with golden cars, is attended by armies of slaves, and earns more than $500,000 a day in oil royalties. He has as yet not accepted any group of refugees for permanent resettlement. The housekeeping cost of Saud's air-conditioned harems and his palace comforts is greater than his nation's educational budget.

Egypt, spurred by the dynamism of social reform, has thrown out the corrupt King Farouk and has substituted for him an aggressive nationalist administration headed by a military junta. It has not offered a haven to any of the 200,000 refugees sweltering in the Gaza strip. This territory, formerly a part of Palestine, was taken by Egypt during the Arab-Israel war; it cannot possibly provide sustenance for even a fraction of the refugees crowded into its narrow area.

Jordan, with an area four times that of Israel, has a population of about 1,500,000, slightly less than that of Israel. When it annexed most of Arab Palestine in 1950, Jordan accepted most of the 465,000 refugees settled there, to whom it has granted citizenship. It is the only Arab country to have done so. The country cannot be

said to be underpopulated, but it is almost wholly un-
derdeveloped. In Biblical days it was the granary of the
Middle East. Today it is disease-ridden; its monarchy is
unstable. An agricultural country, Jordan depends upon
water and trade. Water would be available if Jordan
were to agree to a joint water plan with Israel for
proper use of the Jordan River water. Jordan needs
manufactured materials which it formerly obtained directly from Palestine or from the outside world through
Palestine ports. Hostility between the countries has
terminated trade, and the farmlands of Jordan gain
little from the river. Jordan has stubbornly refused to co-
operate in an irrigation-hydroelectric project, even with
United Nations support, until very recently.

Today Syria, with an area of 66,000 square miles, less
than 15 per cent of it now farmed, has 80,000 refugees
living on its soil. It refuses them the right to find work
and prefers to keep them in refugee camps behind
barbed wire. There would anyway be small incentive to
work; the average Syrian peasant earns about twelve
cents a day. Absentee landlords own large tracts of the
arable acreage; and money lenders' rates of interest im-
poverish the *fellahin*. Tax laws oppress the new peasants
who manage to eke out a little more than bare subsistence; while the rich receive tax concessions from the
government. In the farmhouse where he lives with his
family, the Syrian peasant shares quarters with animals
during the cold months; the villages where he trades
are controlled by local despots who run the local prisons
and the courts. Recently, women were granted partial

political rights. But a woman's full day's work in Syrian industry earns her just about enough to buy a loaf of bread. Polygamy is still practiced; and there are no legal prohibitions against child labor in industry. More than two-thirds of the population is illiterate. To make the country self-sustaining, Syria requires a rural population of 5,000,000; the population is now a little more than 3,000,000. The 80,000 refugees, it is plain to see, could hardly burden the economy; instead they could be a great benefit to it. But the Syrian government, a partner in the Arab League, will not allow the refugees to become contented human beings, if they can be kept as discontented misfits for the world to worry about.

One of the Middle East's potentially most fertile areas is Iraq. Iraq has rich soil, great rivers insuring a plentiful water supply, and tremendous oil and gas reserves to provide dollar royalties, for the purchase of machinery for development. On its 116,000 square miles of territory, Iraq supports a meager population of less than 5,000,000. In Biblical days, when it was known as Mesopotamia, Iraq's land provided a population of an estimated 15,000,000 with a good living. The land nurtured one of the richest nations and one of the most active cultures in the history of the world. Today it is neglected; it needs people. But, on the basis of natural increase, there will never be sufficient population; the average Iraqi dies before he is thirty, half of the children before their fifth birthday. This country could be the granary of the entire Middle East. Yet it finds it impossible to resettle the 4,500 farmer-refugees from Palestine on its soil.

Lebanon, the smallest and the most progressive of the Arab states, has refused to integrate its 108,000 Arab refugees, claiming that it is overpopulated. Actually, Lebanon tills less than a quarter of its 4,000 square miles. The country has an equable climate, good ports, abundant rivers and rainfall, and an intelligent population. The country is, however, half Christian and half Moslem; to accept the refugees, say the Lebanese privately, would unbalance the numerical relationship between Moslem and Christian. Thus, even in enlightened Lebanon, political facts far outweigh human lives.

Assuming that the Arab states would accept the refugees, do the refugees desire resettlement? Propaganda has bewildered them during the last seven years; they are hardly able to know what they want. The Arab leaders tell them to demand nothing but the ultimate; their own land returned with full indemnity for their suffering. They also tell them to hold out; there will be a "second round" and this time the Jews will really "feed the sharks of the Mediterranean." But the refugees are not inclined to believe unquestioningly their avowed benefactors. Promises were made to them in the past and misery ensued. In Arab lands they are prevented from finding secure livelihoods. They know also that those Arabs of Palestine who stayed on while the war raged live now in their old homes, and enjoy prosperity. The refugees have become embittered against their host nations and against cynical promises of all kinds. They resent Israel for not permitting them to return; they refuse to recognize that their squalid homes and sun-baked villages are no more; the old villages, as well as the concentrated Arab quarters in the cities such as Jaffa, have been torn down, rebuilt and resettled. Where once there were mud shacks there are now stone houses. The twisted Arab quarters of the cities have been demolished and in their places have risen new housing developments occupied by Jewish settlers, many of whom migrated from Arab states.

The refugees resent even the United Nations relief organization which feeds and clothes them. In six years, the United Nations has spent more than $240 million in relief for the refugees. There is an additional $200 million fund waiting to be spent for their resettlement, but thus far the Arab nations permit none of it to be disbursed; they just do not want the refugees on Arab soil. Meanwhile the refugees multiply; they increase in number by 25,000 a year, producing more new children with no home and no hope.

A study made by the International Bank for Reconstruction and Development in 1951 observed that the entire refugee problem could be solved within Iraq alone were its resources exploited. It held that, if the Tigris-Euphrates River valley were reclaimed, "several millions of acres of potentially fertile land could be irrigated and a new 'bread basket' created. Perhaps two to three million people could be settled on these new farms. If feasible and carried through . . . the new lands could absorb the seven hundred and fifty thousand Arab refugees from Palestine, at present the gravest source of unrest in the Middle East."

In 1954 a United States Congressional Study Mission visited the Middle East to examine the refugee situation at first hand. In its report to the Foreign Relations Committee of the House, the Mission stated that "the refugees should become citizens of the Arab states and if necessary they should be made wards of the Arab governments pending their admission to citizenship." The Congressmen also urged the United States to "serve notice that it will not support the return of the Arab refugees to their former homes within the boundaries of Israel under existing conditions."

Every kind of reasoning—social, ethnological or economic—shows the feasibility of settling the refugee problem within the vast territory occupied by the Arab nations. Certainly their rehabilitation is a task which Israel alone is unable to accomplish. Israel is ringed by nations whose declared intention is to start another war. To flood the country with hundreds of thousands of potential fifth columnists would constitute an act of national suicide. To take on the economic load of resettling such huge numbers while the nation daily fights insolvency would lead to bankruptcy.

War created the refugee problem. Only a true desire for peace will solve it. This was the cornerstone upon which Abba Eban made his plea before the United Nations in December, 1952. He asked for an attitude of optimism in seeking peace between Israel and her neighbors. All should, he said, with free and open minds, discuss not only the refugee problem, but the blockade, trade agreements, fair division of water resources of the area; social, education and health questions; security questions and intraregional communications, and diplomatic relations. Cooperation such as he enunciated had in fact existed in the recent past, Eban pointed out.

"A few years ago there existed . . . a process of interchange between the Jewish people in Palestine and the neighboring countries. . . . Our . . . population . . . provided a steady and growing market for their agricultural produce and industrial raw materials. . . . Experts of the Hebrew University of Jerusalem went to Iraq to draw up by invitation plans of afforestation and combatting locusts and to organize an entomological service. Emissaries from Iraq were amongst us to investigate commercial organization and rural education. Syria sent workers to study workers' housing. Lebanon dispatched agricultural officials to study methods of botanical research. From all Middle Eastern countries patients flocked to Jerusalem for medical treatment and Jerusalem doctors were called to neighboring capitals for consultations and operations."

Continuing his plea for peace, Eban asked the United Nations that it urge both parties to enter into "free and direct peace negotiations" to achieve rapport "in the proud and venerable area where the arts of civilization were born and whence the call for universal brotherhood came down through the ages to successive generations of men."

# 9 IN DEFENSE OF A FREE WORLD

The geographical location of Israel is, in itself, important enough to warrant the close attention of the Western Powers in their concern for the defense of the Middle East. Israel is a land bridge which unites Asia and Africa. It is the natural focal point, the potential nerve center, for any comprehensive military operation in the region. If the hazards of war paralyze the Suez Canal, Israel affords a short land link between the Mediterranean and the Red Sea—between western and eastern waters. To the north, the land route from Haifa to the Euphrates and thence to the Persian Gulf is the only one to outflank the great mountain ranges which block the Levant from access to the Indian Ocean. Haifa, furthermore, is the one great natural harbor on the Levant coast.

The Haifa-Esdraelon-Euphrates corridor is almost a "water-level route" between the West and the East. Since time out of mind, this route, which Isaiah called the "road to the sea," has been an inevitable highway for the march of great armies. The banners under which these armies have marched—Assyrian, Babylonian, Egyptian, Saracen, or Crusader—have continually changed, but the facts of geography which dictated the line of march have remained the same. These facts cannot be bypassed; nor indeed can Israel for good or ill be bypassed in any conflict which embraces the Middle East.

But Israel offers much more than invaluable geographic advantages. It is the only country in the Middle East with the technical ability to utilize and maintain military equipment on a large scale and to service military forces of any great size. On its own account, it can marshal the best disciplined and most militarily effective body of fighters in the whole region: 350,000 men and women who will fight tenaciously and successfully in the defense of their soil.

In the last world war, when the little country had far from reached its present stage of industrial and agricultural development, the Jewish portion of Palestine—the *Yishuv*—manufactured all the mines used in the decisive struggle at El Alamein. It also supplied the Allied armies with 8,000,000 water and fuel containers; millions more of storage batteries for planes, tanks, trucks and radios; and spare parts of every description for the transportation and communication services. As part of the war effort, Jewish workers and technicians repaired and refitted some 5,000 ships at the port of Haifa. The Dead Sea chemical industry, which was run by Jewish managers and most of whose skilled workers were Jews, was the only source available in the British Empire for the supply of potash and a number of other essential chemical products. Specialists in radio work, in the manufacture of precision and optical instruments, and in a score of fields, which were, and still remain nonexistent in other Middle Eastern countries, helped to make Jewish Palestine's contribution to the world war a notable one. No other country in the Middle East had or even now has the human and industrial resources to make a similar contribution.

Today the contribution could be greater still. Israel owns and operates a first-rate munitions industry, supplemented by plants for the manufacture of precision and other requisite instruments. It has a skilled labor force, an advanced chemical industry, the most efficient communications system in the Middle East, and a large oil refinery. It is no secret that its present army and air force represent a substantial military factor.

But while an army, as Napoleon said, may march on its stomach, it fights on its spirit. The morale of Israel's army is the spirit of Israel itself—that of a free and democratic people prepared to fight for freedom and democracy. As such, it is unique in the Middle East.

Moreover, the defense of the Middle East, as it stands

today and hopefully for the years to come, is not purely or intrinsically a military problem. The Western World is engaged primarily in a conflict of ideas, spiritual values, and human morale. A genuine ally of the West, the only kind of ally that counts in the long run, is one which shares the ideas, values, and morale of western democracy. In the entire Arab world—from Gibraltar to the Khyber Pass—Israel is, almost exclusively and alone, such an ally. Its heart belongs to the West, not only because the Jews have over the centuries absorbed the ideals of the West, but because from Bible days onward they have played a great role in creating those ideals. Peace, justice, the precious rights and freedoms of the individual, were integral to the Israel of the ancient prophets; they have remained integral to an Israel reborn in a struggle for their preservation seven years ago.

In sum, the people of Israel, if we scan their history, have been engaged in the struggle for peace, freedom, and democracy as long as—and in most cases longer than—any other people in western civilization. They will remain constant in that struggle. They can be relied on and should be aided, not because they will respond to favors and rewards, but because they are bound by their own tradition and for their own sake to be true to themselves, that is, to be faithful to the same ideals which we of the West cherish.

To the Western Powers, then, Israel constitutes an irreplaceable, strategic bridge; it is a western, modern country, capable of defending its frontiers with or without allies; and it is potentially a large and efficient arsenal. But first and foremost, Israel, alone in the Middle East, is a free, stable, and democratic nation.

In dealing with the other governments of the Middle East, the dominant Western Powers—Britain, France, and the United States—have never succeeded in making solid progress toward reliable alliances. Relations between the United States and Saudi Arabia, for example, are as fluid as the oil production annually purchased from the Arabian fields; separate King Saud from his oil royalties and he will, like his fathers before him, isolate himself from the "infidels" of the West. The fragility of oil diplomacy was rendered clear in Iran: Mossadegh staked his future on the hatred of his people for the "forcigners." That he overplayed his hand and lost in no way alters the xenophobia on which he gambled.

In Yemen, the hated and despised foreigner is barely allowed to enter the country—and then at his peril. Its absolute ruler, the Imam Saif al Islam Ahmad, controls every department of life. It should, therefore, not be hard to understand that when the Western nations attempt to elicit from these autocrats support for organizations devoted to peace, human rights, and the defense of international law and order, they meet with uncomprehending hostility.

The vast areas of the Middle East are a feature of contemporary maps, but the rulers and inhabitants of these areas are living in centuries which for the West belong to a distant past. It is possible to trade with them —dollars for dates, and pounds for pumped oil; but an interchange of ideas, any genuine communication, is impossible. The gap in time, manners, and traditions is too great. Such countries cannot be allies in any world-wide struggle for democracy; at best they can serve as sullen, contemptuous mercenaries.

The more advanced nations of the region—Iraq, Syria, or Egypt—offer the continuous spectacle of government by riot, exile, and assassination. There is an unending and unedifying round of Farouks, Naguibs, Nassers, Zaims, Shishaklys, and Abdullahs. Elections occasionally take place, but the real balloting is done with dagger and gun. This internal instability presents the Western Powers with a dilemma that is as old as the Arab East. They can extend grants-in-aid, they can donate tractors and harvesters as well as jet planes and Sherman tanks; but in the nature of things they cannot secure what is needed most: a population which understands responsible government and the democratic process, or at least a competent and politically mature ruling class. Without one or the other of these, money, machinery, and modern weapons are wasted on the desert sands. The West so far has never faced up to this dilemma, perhaps on the ostrich theory that by ignoring it, it ceases to exist. Yet if the Middle East is to be won for democracy, something like democracy will have to be introduced into the Middle East. The instrument for this purpose lies, as we shall see, close at hand.

The political orientation of the Arab nations is not so much directed in favor of anything as against it. While their internal policies are reactionary or dictated by factional warfare, their external policies express merely their basic and traditional xenophobia. This was made clear at the Bandung Conference (1955) of Asian and African powers. Much of the oratory at the conference dwelt mainly on the evils of Israel and imperialism. Israel was not invited, but all the Arab nations and Communist China were represented. The Arabs sought by every device to create a bloc committed to the destruction of Israel. To this end they were quite willing to mouth words of praise for the Soviets and words of hatred for the West. They threaten to join hands with the Communists who have repeatedly shown their ill will toward Israel, while at the same time they talk of aligning themselves with the West in a defense pact against the Soviets. It would seem that in the international market, whoever is willing to pay the most can buy the Arabs.

But what is really for sale?

From a military standpoint, the Arab states proved themselves incapable, in their war against Israel, to organize enough strength to defeat a small, poorly armed, and vastly outnumbered enemy. A few years previous to their hapless campaign against Israel, they had already demonstrated not only their military but their moral unfitness to fight in any war which has serious principles at stake. In World War II, Egypt hailed a hoped-for Nazi victory with joy and sympathy; and as the outcome wavered in the long drawn-out duel between Rommel and Montgomery, the British were reduced to maintaining Egyptian loyalty by threat of gunfire. In Iraq (now the beneficiary of American military aid in defense of democracy), Rashid Ali rebelled in favor of the Nazis; today, there is no indication that American or British forces will not at some future date have to reconquer the key Habbaniyah airfield all over again, as the British were compelled to do in the last war. Brigadier Glubb Pasha, commander of the Transjordan Arab Legion, as it was then called, wrote of this episode: "In the six weeks that preceded the fall of Baghdad (in 1941 at the time of the Rashid Ali rebellion) every Arab was convinced that we were finished. Every Arab who had earlier been organized and trained by us rebelled and refused to fight for us or deserted." In Syria, the Arabs fought on the side of the Vichy government and its Nazi masters. Throughout the Near East, Allied pipelines and communication lines were sabotaged by Arabs. Many of these anti-democratic manifestations might have been a surprise to the Western Powers in the 1940's—though T. E. Lawrence warned them that Arabs will fight only for loot and when victory seems sure. But today, after repeated cynical avowals on the part of Arab statesmen and governors, new treacheries would be due to Western stupidity or willful obstinacy.

The lesson of the last war in the Middle East resolves itself to one simple fact: the British and Anzacs had to operate as "occupation troops" in countries that were supposed to be their allies in the war against Nazism. Such being the case, it was an act of folly to arm these presumed "allies" at the beginning in order to fight them at the end. Fortunately, just because the Egyptians, Iraqis, and Syrians turned out to be poor and inefficient fighters, this absurd procedure did not end in disaster. Perhaps it will not prove disastrous next time for the same reasons, but meanwhile it may be hoped that our Allied strategists, if they are not immune to common sense, will become aware of what has been demonstrated to be a waste of money and arms.

Vivid proof of what the struggle for democracy means to Israel, in contrast to the Arab states, was to be seen in the celebration in 1955 of the tenth anniversary of Israel's (or Jewish Palestine's) participation in World War II. Parades, speeches, radio programs, solemn rites and memorial occasions recalled and consecrated Israel's part in the war against the Nazis—against, that is, the tyranny over mind and body which is the antithesis of democracy. No such celebration was held, still less contemplated, in any Arab country. It may be advanced, and rightly, that Israel and the Jews had especially good reason to combat Nazism and celebrate their part in its downfall. But this in turn simply means that Israel and the Jews have become, through tragic experience, more dedicated than ever to the cause which America and her Western Allies are now upholding. Because they are more dedicated, they are surely the more loyal and effective allies.

Today, as in the past, Arab unity is a myth; the Arab potentates hate one another in their struggle for power as much as they detest Israel. The Hashemite dynasties (Iraq and Jordan) are pitted against Saudi Arabia and

Egypt; each group maneuvers for dominance; Syria plots for a "Greater Syria" at the expense of its Arab neighbors. Besides, these lands of "Arab unity" are full of discontented and approved minorities: Kurds, Copts, Druses, Maronite Christians, and the like. The Arab League, once the presumed expression of "unity," flourished only until it met its first real test in the war against Israel; each of its five armies fought on their own and for their own, and—because of internecine jealousies— never at the same time. They were more absorbed in denying victory to one another than to Israel, and the final triumph of the latter exposed the inherent weakness of the League.

The Arab nations, however, remain united in one respect: they all recognize in Israel a threat to the political and social feudalism on which the power of their leaders is based. The example which Israel sets of a genuinely democratic society does in fact menace the selfish privileges and the means of exploitation enjoyed by the *effendis*, the *pashas*, and the military *juntas*. To the extent that they are permitted to see and know something of Israel's democracy, the downtrodden *fellahin* will be spurred into making troublesome demands for a better life.

By overwhelming Israel, the Arab rulers hope to destroy this potential source of trouble. This hope, which has reached the intensity of an obsession, has blinded their sense of reality. Israel, perhaps, might vanish in defeat and with it the sole democratic society in the

Middle East; but it is an illusion to believe that feudalism would thereafter be left to stagnate at will. Soviet agents are already at work in the villages and refugee camps, presenting a far greater menace to their autocratic rule than the progressive policy of a free, liberal, and dynamic Israel. Israel seeks nothing but peace and progress; the Communists offer nothing but false promises and their victory would end any Arab hopes for a real improvement in living conditions in the Middle East.

What then is the solution—for Arab, Jew, and the Western Powers? There is but one, and that is to prevail upon the Arabs to make peace with Israel. None of the issues which separate the two parties is incapable of compromise and adjustment, once the Arabs concede the existence of Israel and the basic requisites for this existence, and once the Arabs are induced to wish, plan, and act for peace. Next, the Arabs must improve the lot of their own people by using their huge oil revenues to develop Arab lands and raise their standards of education, health, and economic well-being. In these efforts the United Nations and the United States have declared their willingness to play a substantial role.

Such a program—and not the grant of armaments—will assure the future of the Arab nations. The Western Powers should be particularly eager to foster this program, for as we have said, the world conflict today is a battle for the minds of men and their way of life. As for Israel, such a program, grounded as it is on peace, will

be the solution of its gravest economic difficulties. Once
the Arab blockade is lifted and the trade of the region
allowed to take its natural course, Israel will be assured
of a plentiful supply of food and the Arab neighbors of
manufactured goods at low, normal prices. In an era
of peaceful commerce and of a common effort toward
improving the general welfare, the waters of the Jordan
and Yarmuk rivers, as well as of the Litani, could be
harnessed for the development of hydraulic power and
irrigation sorely needed by the entire region. Toward
this comprehensive and beneficent goal—peace and
plenty—Moshe Sharett, the second prime minister of
Israel, has declared that his country is prepared to offer
the Arab states a hundred-year nonaggression pact. The
result could be nothing less than a reign of unparalleled
prosperity in the Near East.

The prospects opened by this program ought to be
especially attractive to America. In the Marshall Aid
and Point Four programs, the American State Department has repeatedly proclaimed that it was supporting
democracy with dollars. This in fact has been done in
Western Europe, where democracy already existed. The
problem, although not the goal, is quite different in
nondemocratic lands such as the Arab states. There the
United States can send over machinery, technical experts, foodstuffs, and cash; but it cannot supply these
nations with democracy.

Theodor Herzl once said, as an expression of his Zionism, that "whoever wishes to change men must change

the conditions under which they live." Grants under Mutual Aid and Point Four can help furnish the means for changing conditions in Arab lands, but the conditions are bound to remain much the same as in the past unless and until the Arabs themselves have the *will* to make them different. Precepts can do little, examples can do much more, and close contacts can do most of all toward cultivating among the Arabs the required determination to enter upon a free, full, and democratic life.

It is at this point that Israel can render a unique service to America in its efforts to win the Middle East to the democratic cause, to make of that region not merely a military air base and an oil reservoir but an integral part of the free world. No other nation is in a position to render this service. When it comes to exemplary action, America itself is too remote. The people of the underprivileged countries in the Near East may well say to American exponents of a better life, "Yes, that is all very well for you in your vast country with its huge resources. But in our small and poor land, it won't work." America in truth is richly blessed; but it is also true that Israel, the immediate neighbor of these impoverished and backward Arab lands, is tiny and devoid of great natural wealth. The American exponents of democracy could therefore answer, "Look at Israel's success! Democracy in Israel produces health, freedom, and prosperity, whereas communism or feudalism in other lands ends in economic enslavement and political death."

The young republic of Israel can thus be democracy's test case and showcase in the Middle East.

If the United States and the other Western Powers who have a vital stake in raising the standards of the Middle East would induce the Arabs to enter into peaceful relations with Israel, the friendly, normal contacts which would ensue between Israel and its neighbors would, in the course of time, result in countless benefits to both.

One small but significant example of what free and friendly contacts may do is seen in the recent visit of the premier of Burma to Israel. After inspecting a number of the communal settlements (*kibbutzim*) in the Emek and the Jordan Valley, Premier Nu said, "I believe that the life lived in a *kibbutz* can be the life lived in Burma according to the principles of Buddhism," and he proposed to apply the *kibbutz* system to his own country.

Once normal intercourse is established between Israel and the Arab nations, and Israeli Arabs come to know from personal experience that the human merits and the material benefits of democracy can circulate freely among their kindred abroad, the pace of progress will be enormously hastened. Israel will become not only the showcase but the salesman of democracy. The profits from this particular kind of commerce will be shared by all liberty-loving men.

Meanwhile, whether encouraged or not by the Western Powers to fulfill its obvious function in the Middle East, Israel will continue to serve the world by heartening idealists everywhere. The little land stands as a testimony to the optimistic creative spirit of mankind. It proves that even in an age shattered by war and betrayed by false messiahs, the great dreams of man can still come true.

# 10 "HOUSE OF OUR LIFE"

An ancient Jewish blessing which follows the weekly reading from the Prophets in the synagogue service speaks of Zion as the "house of our life." In these few words, the author of this blessing describes what Zion has meant to the Jew throughout his millenial history.

Exiled from his own land, driven from one corner of the world to another, the Jew continued to dwell in the "house" of his life. For him it was a house filled with the memories and hopes, the history and faith of his people. Therein lay the secret of Jewish survival.

Study, prayer, and continuous yearning fashioned for the Jews this unique spiritual link with Zion. The past was lived and relived by them in liturgy and song, on the Sabbath and holy days. At every season each feast evoked a fragment, a mood, or an episode of the lost life of that land. Throughout the centuries, the joys and sorrows they encountered in their daily existence, the prayers they intoned, the garments they wore, the food they ate and the calendar they used—all these re- called to the Jews the life of ancient Zion. Thus they learned to defy the present.

Other peoples, scattered abroad by ill fate, found a home in the present and gave up their identity and cul- tural integrity. Not so the Jews. Throughout the ages they refused to deny their past and make peace with the present. Prevented from living a life of Jewish dignity in the present, they turned to their past and lived in its history. It was a history which spoke of a land few of them ever saw, a language few spoke, and glories they never knew. Nevertheless, they lived in it, for in it they found the promise for the future.

Now that the Jews have recovered the land, these ties to the past have not lost their significance by virtue of a happier present, but rather have been strengthened and the obligations they entail reaffirmed.

The nightmare of an interminable exile is over. The Jewish people, as a national entity, was in exile so long as it possessed no land or state of its own. Today, the Jewish people has a land and a state. For large numbers of Jews who do not live in Israel, the fact of continued settlement outside of Israel in no way implies a state of exile. As Marvin Lowenthal put it: "The Jews of Soviet Russia who wish to go to Israel and can't, are not exiles, but prisoners. The Jews of America and elsewhere who can go to Israel but don't, are not exiles, but Jewish settlers of one or many generations in the world at large, as much justified in their choice of flag and country as any other human being."

Since the dream of rebuilding Zion never envisioned the total immigration of *all* the Jews to Israel, the continued existence of Jewish communities outside Israel does not negate the Zionist ideal. Indeed, if total immigration had been the objective, any economist could have foretold that Palestine was *not* the place. As far back as the first century of the common era, Philo, the Jewish philosopher, wrote that "no one country can contain the whole Jewish nation, by reason of its numbers, on account of which they inhabit all the . . . lands of Europe and Asia . . . looking indeed upon the holy city [of Jerusalem] as their metropolis, in which is erected the sacred temple of the most high God." During the latter days of the Second Commonwealth, twice as many Jews lived outside as inside the boundaries of Palestine. Today, even optimistic estimates grant that a population of 3,500,000 would strain the country's resources. Yet more than 5,000,000 Jews live in the United States alone. If all the Jews of the world wished to settle in Israel, the country could not accommodate them.

Theodor Herzl explicitly declared at the First Zionist Congress (1897): "Nowhere can there be a question of the exodus of all the Jews. Those who are able or wish to [remain] will stay behind." Zionism has not sought the impossible and, for many persons, the undesirable goal of transferring all Jews, individuals and communities alike, to Israel. Zionism has rather pursued the noble aim of rebuilding there the "house of our life," which, as a free and flourishing Jewish state, will be a source of inspiration and renewed values for world Jewry. Israel is not simply a shelter, but a house and a source of life.

Once again the Jewish people enjoys, through the resettlement and liberation of its own land, a place and a destiny among the nations. What has this achievement meant, in these first few years of Israel's renewed existence, to Jews everywhere?

First and most important is the fact that to every Jew Israel offers a home. This means that Jews, like all men, may feel that wherever they dwell, it is by choice and not of necessity. The right to choose one's domicile is inherent in Freedom, and Israel has brought this right to the Jews. None can now say: "You're here because you have no other place; therefore, you must be tolerated."

Second, the creation of Israel resulted in encouraging the development of the Hebrew language, in a fresh and keener understanding of Jewish history, and in an active appreciation of Jewish art, music, drama and literature. This release of spiritual energy and initiative has stimulated in every part of the Jewish world the beginning of a magnificent renaissance of Jewish culture.

Third, Israel offers to every Jew more than the opportunity to make a choice and more than cultural rebirth. The comfort of knowing that his people has struck roots somewhere in the world and that it is playing its own role among the family of nations provides the Jew, wherever he may be, with a sense of normalcy. This reassurance, in turn, should help him cast off his hypersensitive preoccupation with self-defense, the morbid negative side of combatting anti-Semitism. Proud of Jewish achievement in Israel, and determined that his own life shall be more worthy of the Jewish past, many a Jew for the first time will discover joy in what previously had been a burden.

Beyond the necessity for the physical creation of a state, Zionist leaders never lost sight of the high ideals and the lofty principles upon which a Jewish state must be based. In the early days of political Zionism, Theodor Herzl envisaged the new Zion as a land "where we shall live at peace with all the world, which we have freed through our freedom, enriched by our wealth, and made greater by our own greatness." He visualized it as a land where "by means of our state we can educate our people for the tasks which still lie beyond our ken. For God would not have kept us alive so long if there were not left for us a role to play in the history of mankind." Herzl was simply echoing the ancient prophetic vision of a land where righteousness shall well forth as a mighty stream. The prophets, in turn, echoed the divine admonition to Abraham that the land he will inherit shall not only be blessed in itself but shall be one through which all the peoples of the earth shall be blessed, thus fulfilling the prophecy of Isaiah that "out of Zion shall go forth the Law and the Word of the Lord from Jerusalem."

Upon this ancient vision, the very foundation of Jewish existence, was built the Zionist resolve that, given the chance in a land of their own, Jews will "do justly, love mercy, and walk humbly with [their] God."

In the final chapter of his autobiography, Chaim Weizmann described Israel's goal as "the building of a high civilization based on the austere standards of Jewish ethics. From these standards we must not swerve." The Jews, he continued, must "center their activities on genuine values, whether in industry, agriculture, science, literature or art." Weizmann further maintained that "Palestine will have to produce quality goods . . . The production of quality goods is not merely a matter of skill. It is also based on an honest relationship to the task in hand."

To Weizmann, the dedicated scientist, "quality goods" transcended the purely material aspects of the product. "Science to him," says Maurice Samuel, "was . . . a thing of character no less than of aptitudes, a builder of men and of a tradition, no less than of knowledge, power, and goods." Moreover, "in the creation of a model of prototype, the Jews of the world, drawing on the best of western democracy, were to be equal partners with the Jews of the homeland."

Seven years of independence, or even the two generations of pioneering and building which preceded the establishment of the Jewish state, are naturally but a brief fragment of the time required for any people to settle a land, to win freedom, and to make an outstanding contribution to civilization. After three centuries, and despite great material achievement, Americans are still struggling to fulfill the American dream. Nonetheless, the people of Israel can take honest pride in what they have already accomplished, a pride to be legitimately shared by all Jews, wherever they are, who have lent a hand or a thought to the work.

The Jews of other lands cannot share in the thrill of upbuilding Israel or derive from it the inspiration to which they are entitled, without some substantial effort on their own part. They must strengthen the bond of fellowship between themselves and the Jews of Israel, and commit themselves along with them to the common task of making the ideals of Judaism come true.

The common loyalty which American Jews and Israelis share is a loyalty to the institutions, ideals, and aspirations of the Jewish people. In other words, a loyalty to Judaism in the broadest sense of the term. Justice Brandeis wrote: "There is no inconsistency between loyalty to America and loyalty to Jewry. The Jewish spirit, the product of our religion and experiences, is essentially modern and essentially American . . . Indeed, loyalty to America demands rather that each American Jew becomes a Zionist. For only through the ennobling effect of its strivings can we develop the best that is in us and give to this country the full benefit of our inheritance."

American Jews who visit Israel return more dedicated as Jews and no less dedicated as Americans. Even those who are unable to make the journey but steep themselves in Israeli culture through the media of literature, art and music become enriched in spirit. The American Jew, young or old, who has dwelt, however briefly, in the "house of our life" which is Zion—be it the real Zion in Israel, or the intangible Zion reconstructed from knowledge, love, and devotion—will find his own life much more vigorous and far more meaningful.

This is a fact of deepest significance. This alone justifies the undying longing of an ancient people for their land. Above all, it is this which makes the present so pre-eminently a time for hopefulness for every thinking Jew who sees in Israel the eternal ideal of his people.

In the tractate *Megilla* are to be found these prophetic words: "This people [Jewry] is likened to the dust and the stars. When they go down they go down to the very dust. But when they rise, they rise up to the stars."

## SELECTED READINGS

### HISTORY OF THE JEWS

Graetz, Heinrich, *History of the Jews*, Philadelphia, Jewish Publication Society, 1927; 6 vols.

Elbogen, Ismar, *A Century of Jewish Life*, Philadelphia, Jewish Publication Society, 1944.

Baron, Salo, *A Social and Religious History of the Jews*, Philadelphia, Jewish Publication Society, 1952; 3 vols.

### HISTORY OF PALESTINE

Locker, Berl, *Covenant Everlasting: Palestine in Jewish History*, New York, Sharon Books, 1947.

Parkes, James, *History of Palestine: 139 A.D. to Modern Times*, New York Oxford University Press, 1949.

Revusky, Abraham, *Jews in Palestine*, New York, Vanguard Press, 1945.


ZIONISM

Herzl, Theodor, *The Jewish State*, New York, American Zionist Emergency Council, 1946.

Bein, Alexander, *Theodor Herzl, a Biography*, Philadelphia, Jewish Publication Society, 1940.

Weizmann, Chaim, *Trial and Error*, New York, Harper and Brothers, 1949.

Learsi, Rufus, *Fulfillment: the Epic Story of Zionism*, Cleveland and New York World Publishing Company, 1951.

Cohen, Israel, *The Zionist Movement*, New York, Zionist Organization of America, 1946.

Samuel, Maurice, *Harvest in the Desert*, Philadelphia, Jewish Publication Society, 1944.


ISRAEL, EMERGENCE AND DEVELOPMENT

Eban, Abba, *Modern Israel—an Adventure in the Human Spirit*, University of Notre Dame, South Bend, Indiana, 1955.

Dunner, Joseph, *The Republic of Israel*, New York, Whittlesey House, 1950.

Hobman, J. S., *Palestine's Economic Future: a Review of Progress and Prospects*, London, Lind Humphries, 1948.

Huebner, Theodore, *Education in Israel*, New York, The Modern Language Journal, December 1953.

Halkin, Simon, *Modern Hebrew Literature: Trends and Values*, New York, Schocken Books, 1950.

ARAB REFUGEES

Eban, Abba, *The Arab Refugees*, United Nations, New York, October 1952.

Comay, Michael, *The Future of the Arab Refugees*, Israel Office of Information, New York, 1953.

Khan, Mizra, *Arab Propaganda in the United States*, Jewish Frontier, October-November 1953.

Government of Israel, *The Arab Refugees*, Jerusalem, 1953.

# INDEX